Transfo

Realising

CABI: Who we are and what we do

This book is published by CABI, an international not-for-profit organization that improves people's lives worldwide by providing information and applying scientific expertise to solve problems in agriculture and the environment.

CABI is also a global publisher producing key scientific publications, including the world renowned CAB Abstracts (the leading abstracting and indexing database in the applied life sciences), Global Health (a specialist bibliographic abstracting and indexing database dedicated to public health), as well as compendia, books, ebooks and full text electronic resources. We publish content in a wide range of subject areas including:

- agriculture and crop science
- animal and veterinary sciences
- ecology and conservation
- environmental science
- horticulture and plant sciences
- human health, food science and nutrition
- international development
- leisure and tourism

The profits from CABI's publishing activities enable us to work with farming communities around the world, supporting them as they battle with poor soil, invasive species and pests and diseases, to improve their livelihoods and help provide food for an ever growing population.

CABI is an international intergovernmental organisation and we gratefully acknowledge the core financial support from our member countries (and lead agencies) including the United Kingdom (Department for International Development), China (Chinese Ministry of Agriculture), Australia (Australian Centre for International Agricultural Research), Canada (Agriculture and Agri-Food Canada), Netherlands (Directorate-General for International Cooperation), and Switzerland (Swiss Agency for Development and Cooperation).

Discover more

To read more about CABI's work, please visit **www.cabi.org**

Browse our books at **www.cabi.org/bookshop**, or explore our online products at **www.cabi.org/publishing-products**

Interested in writing for CABI? Find our author guidelines here: **www.cabi.org/publishing-products/information-for-authors/**

Transforming Travel
Realising the potential of sustainable tourism

Jeremy Smith

CABI is a trading name of CAB International

CABI
Nosworthy Way
Wallingford
Oxfordshire OX10 8DE
UK

Tel: +44 (0)1491 832111
Fax: +44 (0)1491 833508
E-mail: info@cabi.org
Website: www.cabi.org

CABI
745 Atlantic Avenue
8th Floor
Boston, MA 02111
USA

Tel: +1 (617)682-9015
E-mail: cabi-nao@cabi.org

A catalogue record for this book is available from the British Library, London, UK.

ISBN-13: 9781786394194 (pbk)
9781786394200 (PDF)
9781786394217 (ePub)

Commissioning editor: Claire Parfitt
Associate editor: Alexandra Lainsbury
Production editor: Tim Kapp

Typeset by SPi, Pondicherry, India
Printed and bound in the UK by Bell & Bain Ltd, Glasgow, G46 7UQ

Contents

To access a presentation delivered by Jeremy Smith
and also an interview with him, please visit:
http://www.cabi.org/openresources/94194/

Acknowledgements

My thanks to Claire Parfitt and the team at CABI for making it possible to write the book I wanted to, and to do so for a publisher with a non-profit, social-impact focussed way of operating. To Anula Galewska and all of my friends and colleagues at Travindy for our collaborations so far. To the teams at WTM and WTTC for the continuing chance to write and explore my ideas over the last few years. And to Gail Perkins, Sally Davey, Xavier Font, Irena Ateljevic, Vicky Smith, Anna Pollock, Gopi Parayil, Anke Winchenbach, Ellie Cleary, Daniel Elkan, Ben Salt, Ayako Ezaki, Ian Ord, Gregorio Rojas, and many others for their suggestions for making this a better book than I could have managed alone.

Amid all the doom-laden exhortations to change our ways, let us remember that we are striving to create a more beautiful world, and not sustain, with growing sacrifice, the current one. We are not just seeking to survive. We are not just facing doom; we are facing a glorious possibility. We are offering people not a world of less, not a world of sacrifice, not a world where you are just going to have to enjoy less and suffer more – no, we are offering a world of more beauty, more joy, more connection, more love, more fulfillment, more exuberance, more leisure, more music, more dancing, and more celebration. The most inspiring glimpses you've ever had about what human life can be – that is what we are offering.

Charles Eisenstein

Awaken people's curiosity. It is enough to open minds; do not overload them. Put there just a spark. If there is some good flammable stuff, it will catch fire.

Anatole France

Foreword

We are at a pivotal moment in the tourism industry.

In a world where overtourism has gotten so bad that it's causing riots around the world, where the industry accounts for nearly 12% of global carbon emissions, and more tourism dollars are flowing outside of local communities than into them, it almost seems that the rapidly growing and ever-popular travel industry is a beast that cannot be controlled.

But there is another story. One of hope and determination. One where tourism – something so universally appealing and almost too simple a solution – has the potential to help alleviate poverty, close the gender gap, build a more environmentally resilient world, and so much more.

The latter is the story Jeremy shares.

When I started building Impact Travel Alliance, which has now become the world's largest community for mindful travel professionals, I had no idea how quickly the grassroots movement would take off. In less than three years, we have grown to more than 15,000 members worldwide, with local teams run by about 250 volunteers, in 25 cities around the world. As I've witnessed our local chapters come to life, I've been in a unique position to see a birds' eye view of visionaries around the world and throughout our industry.

ITA's growth is due to the same passions and phenomena that Jeremy showcases in the following pages. Innovators – from start-up representatives to those in the corporate world – are dedicated to building a brighter future for our industry.

Jeremy's book puts pen to paper for the action I've seen throughout ITA's community, and shares actionable insight and inspiration to apply to your own business. The examples he showcases provide a collection of fresh insights on how to push our industry forward, and I'm confident they will motivate you to action.

Through Jeremy's thoughtful and progressive analysis of the industry, as woven throughout stories and examples from around the world, you can begin to understand why sustainable travel is the future of the industry. It holds the key to more meaningful experiences for travellers and lasting contributions to the destinations visited. But in order to build this world, we must shift how we view sustainable tourism. The time is now to take action, and this book offers us a roadmap to begin to take these steps.

Transforming Travel offers a story of hope. It plants the seeds to push our industry forward, and if you believe in the possibility of improving our world through travel, it is a must-read.

I hope you will enjoy reading it as much as I did.

Warmly,
Kelley Louise
Executive Director
Impact Travel Alliance

Preface

Spread either side of the dirt road that clatters from Morondava to Belon'i Tsiribihina, the 25 immense trees known together as the Avenue des Baobabs are definitely worth the journey. The Malagasy people call them *renala*, the Mother of the Forest. To me and the other tourists they are Grandidier baobabs, named after the French botanist Alfred Grandidier, but nonetheless the grandest of them all.

Like most visitors to the island, I have come to witness sunset at 'the most iconic destination in Madagascar'. Sipping slowly from a warmish bottle of Three Horses Beer, I amble back and forth across the scrubby land between these 30-metre giants, seeking the best position for my photo – maximum number of trees set against minimal number of other tourists.

Malagasy legend says the trees were turned upside down in punishment for being too proud of their own beauty. Or maybe it was that when God created the baobabs as the Earth's first trees, he accidentally planted them upside down? As the baobabs have lived here for around 1000 years, there's been plenty of time for tall tales.

The truth, however, is altogether less romantic. Ninety per cent of Madagascar's original tree cover has been cut down, half in the last 50 years. The baobab survives because her bark is so light that while she may look beautiful to tourists, she is useless to loggers. The ancient Mother of the Forest stands alone because the forest around her has been cleared.

'A way of seeing is also a way of not seeing', wrote literary theorist Kenneth Burke. 'A focus upon object A involves a neglect of object B'. You either see the wood. Or you see the trees.

But this is rarely the story the brochures tell. The Avenue des Baobabs is sold and celebrated as a bucket-list destination, an awesome sunset spot to share on Instagram. Few tourists come here and also contemplate the absence that makes the shot possible.

Does it have to be this way? One or the other. What if we could build a tourism industry that celebrates the beauty we see around us, without ignoring whatever it took to create it? Could we go even further, and reimagine

this industry as one that revives us when we travel, and does so through restoring the world we visit?

Let's sow a few seeds.

Introduction

Ten years ago, I spent nine months journeying across the world while researching a guidebook on sustainable tourism. I took the train from London to Hanoi. Got sore on a Mongolian horse with a wooden saddle. Sipped sweet chai on the deck of the Rocket ferry in Bangladesh while Gangetic dolphins rode the bow waves beneath. Slept in five-star treehouse luxury in South Africa, and in the spare room of a Thai family whose village had almost been wiped out by a tsunami.

For most of the time since, I have focused on talking to the travel industry. I am the editor and co-founder of Travindy, the only B2B news site that deals exclusively with issues around tourism and sustainability. I write a fortnightly blog for World Travel Market on these subjects, and produce the World Travel and Tourism Council's monthly Tourism for Tomorrow newsletter. I also work with organizations and companies ranging from a national park and international trade bodies to independent lodges and tour companies, helping them better communicate their efforts to run tourism as sustainably and equitably as they can.

Ten years ago, when I set off to write that first guidebook, I'd done very little work in this industry. In April 2007, I had stepped down as editor of *The Ecologist*, which was then the world's longest running environmental magazine. I'd been there for six years, covering just about every topic relating to development and our impact on the environment. What I learned there had a lasting impact on how I see the world. But I'd always struggled with the magazine's established editorial position on tourism, which was unremittingly negative. When the UN declared 2002 the International Year for Ecotourism, for example, we were highly critical. From then on, on the very few occasions that we published anything on tourism, this remained our stance.

I'd done very little work on the subject, but I'd spent a lot of time being a tourist. I therefore needed to resolve the conflict between my magazine's editorial position and my personal experience that travel had been good for how I related to the world, its peoples and its environment. Researching and writing that first travel guide was partly an attempt to settle this dilemma, and it convinced me that there was enormous, perhaps unrivalled, potential inside of this industry.

Ten years later I still believe this. However, the ensuing decade has also shown me that my confusion about what tourism should be, and how it might be a force for good, is far from unique. Everywhere I look I see doubt and contradiction about the industry's purpose, and what it will take to deliver on its potential. This book explores the reasons for this dilemma, and offers a new way forward.

Why is tourism confused?

Many say that tourism is the largest service industry on earth. The two figures most often cited to support this claim are that it is responsible for 10% of GDP and one in ten jobs. Importantly, these numbers don't come from tourism's direct impact or the number of people directly employed in the industry, but by adding in the indirect and induced contributions of the many players in its supply chain as well, from the people who grow the food or those who pick up visitors from airports all the way to the induced spending on our pets stimulated by tourism. As the World Travel and Tourism Council (WTTC) explains:

> In 2016, Travel & Tourism directly contributed US$2.3 trillion and 109 million jobs worldwide. Taking its wider indirect and induced impacts into account, the sector contributed US$7.6 trillion to the global economy and supported 292 million jobs in 2016. This was equal to 10.2% of the world's GDP, and approximately 1 in 10 of all jobs.[1]

In 2002, the International Year of Ecotourism, there were 698 million international tourist arrivals. By 2007, the year I began work on the guidebook, the number had risen to 911 million. In 2015, there were 1.186 billion international arrivals. By 2030, the UN's World Tourism Organization (UNWTO) has projected the number of international tourist arrivals will increase by a further 50%, reaching more than 1.8 billion. Don't be surprised if it isn't considerably more.

These international numbers only tell a small part of the story. According to the UNTWO:

> tourist spending swelled from only $2 billion in 1950 to $1.2 trillion in 2015. The number of international tourists has grown by orders of magnitude as well, from 25 million traveled in 1950 to 1.2 billion in 2015. Domestic tourism is even bigger. It is estimated that between 5 and 6 billion people take holidays at home. In one way or another, we are almost all tourists.[2]

---

[1] https://www.wttc.org/-/media/files/reports/economic-impact-research/2017-documents/global-economic-impact-and-issues-2017.pdf (accessed 4 August 2017).
[2] https://www.devex.com/news/opinion-packing-your-bags-here-are-4-ways-to-become-a-sustainable-tourist-90542 (accessed 27 July 2017).

However they are reached, these figures depict an industry that is growing remarkably fast and generating a huge amount of money. Yet they only paint a partial picture. Because while the division between an international tourist and a domestic one is simple enough, actually defining who are tourists, and therefore factoring their impact into our planning, is considerably harder.

The UNWTO states:

> Tourism is defined as the activities of persons identified as visitors. A visitor is someone who is making a visit to a main destination outside his/her usual environment for less than a year for any main purpose [including] holidays, leisure and recreation, business, health, education or other purposes.[3]

Even this extremely broad definition has its limits. If I go and use the same services as visiting tourists in my home city of London, I am not a tourist, yet I'm contributing the same money into the same parts of the economy. And I'm adding the same pressures. Some 4.5 million people were said to visit the food stalls, cafes and bars of London's Borough Market in 2011. But how many were locals sourcing vegetables as ingredients, how many were visitors perhaps buying lunch or snacks, and how many were simply there as sightseers?

All of us made the market more crowded. All of us put pressure on the logistics of running the place, and created waste, consumed water, relied on electricity. And we all handed over money in the same currency to the traders and restaurateurs.

Does the split between visitor and local tell the full story? Which segment should the market be doing the most to look after and attract? Whose economic impact is most valuable? A 2011 article in *Wanderlust* magazine quotes one of the market traders:

> There are loads of tourists but they don't necessarily spend any money [...]. I'm sure it's in all the Rough Guides to London – it's a tourist attraction basically. It can get a bit annoying when they're just standing there taking photos.

Why are people getting a 'bit annoyed'?

There are protests against mega tourism developments in Bali. Groups resisting airport development everywhere from London to Tokyo. Graffiti has been scrawled across walls in Europe reading 'Refugees Welcome. Tourists Go Home', and in the summer of 2017 a tourist bus in Barcelona was surrounded and the words 'tourism kills neighbourhoods' sprayed (in Catalan) on the windscreen. Venice has seen local people throw flares, take to boats and swim out into the Grand Canal to protest ever-growing numbers of

---

[3] http://www.tourismsociety.org/page/88/tourism-definitions.htm (accessed 30 May 2017).

Fig. 1.1. Graffiti such as this has been appearing with increasing regularity across walls in Europe.

ever-larger cruise ships. It is so bad in the city that UNESCO is considering removing its World Heritage site status. There's even a neologism specifically penned for these growth pains – 'Overtourism', a word whose own overuse is so anticipated that it has already been trademarked by the website where it first appeared, Skift.

As well as the effect these crowds have on people's livelihoods and well-being, this constant growth is also having a negative effect on the environment. According the UNWTO's previous Director General Taleb Rifai, in a 2017 article written with Erik Solheim and Patricia Espinosa on the Devex development website: 'Tourism generates an estimated 5 percent of global greenhouse gas emissions.' This is the figure the industry uses most often. However, the same article continues: 'According to U.N. Environment, that proportion is higher – 12.5 percent – if factors such as energy use at hotels and transporting food and toiletries are included.' Considering the industry routinely claims it is responsible for one in ten jobs, factoring in its supply chain when promoting its importance, then it follows that the supply chain has to be factored in when calculating its impact. Dr Susanne Becken is one of the two lead researchers for the Global Sustainable Tourism Dashboard, which uses the industry's own data to establish an accurate picture of its impact on global development. As she sees it: 'One can only compare apples with apples, so if we look at direct emissions (as in the 5% attempt), then one can only juxtapose it with direct economic impact.'[4]

---

[4] Personal correspondence 6 August 2017.

Not only is its environmental impact 150% greater than the industry tends to acknowledge, it is also predicted to get a lot worse. In 2015, the world's two leading scientists studying tourism and climate change published a damning article in the *Journal of Sustainable Tourism*, which stated that 'the global tourism system is increasingly at odds with objectives to reduce global resource use'. According to authors Stefan Gossling and Paul Peeters, whichever way you look at it, tourism's growth is becoming ever more unsustainable. The article found that if tourism carries on with a 'business-as-usual scenario' then it is set to double its energy use over the coming 25 years. It will also double its land use over the same period. Water use won't rise so quickly, but in 45 years the industry's use of that will have doubled too.

This predicted growth will take place across the same time frame that the world has committed to reduce its impact in an attempt to keep global temperature rises within liveable thresholds. During this period, the developing impacts of climate change will also be putting ever-greater pressure on both land and water. Some 24% of India's arable land is already turning to desert. To the north, in China, desertification is already causing annual losses of US$65 billion. And while the heat dries some regions, in others it causes floods. The rivers that start in the ice of the Himalayan mountains that stand between these two vast nations sustain 46% of the world's population. Yet in 2008 it was discovered that the region's glaciers had already lost all the ice formed since the mid-1940s, and it is estimated that one third of them will be gone by 2050. The European Alps have lost half the glacier cover they had a century ago. Around the world, sea levels rose about 8 inches in the last century, with the rate in the last two decades being nearly twice as fast as before.[5]

Everywhere one looks, from melting alpine snows to bleached coral reefs and rising seas, the natural world upon which so much tourism depends is being threatened by the consequences of fossil-fuelled human development. How the industry chooses to respond will define its future.

How is the tourism industry responding?

The standard response to dealing with social and environmental challenges is an incremental one. Thomas Cook's 2015 sustainability report states that its objective is to 'make every holiday more sustainable and drive incremental change'.[6] Likewise, according to Wyndham's latest corporate social responsibility report, onsite solar represents 0.08% of the company's energy production. In the report, Wyndham states that its targets include: 'Generate

---

[5] https://climate.nasa.gov/evidence/ (accessed 29 July 2017).
[6] https://www.thomascookgroup.com/wp-content/uploads/2016/01/Sustainability-Report-2015.pdf (accessed 29 July 2017).

10% of total electricity through onsite renewable energy by 2035'. That's an increase of around 0.5% a year.

The argument for such incrementalism is that it is easier to get people (be they customers, staff or shareholders) to engage with, because it involves less dramatic – transformative – change. Whether it's getting people to hang up their towels a bit more often, or committing your airline to a 1% annual reduction in emissions, such efforts require less radical action and so are more likely to happen. It follows that succeeding in them generates a positive feeling of achievement – of the very do-ability of an action, which then motivates one, or one's organization, to make incrementally greater change. We start slow, but we gather pace. 'This veneer environmentalism complements and rein-forces the opportunistic environmentalism of industry', writes David Weaver, Professor of Tourism Research at Griffith University, 'and constitutes perhaps a parallel process of "consumer behavioural nudge" that will also help to gradually push the sector to higher levels of sustainability engagement.'[7]

Not everyone agrees with this approach. When it comes to addressing increasingly urgent issues such as global warming and its impacts, others argue that the time for incremental change has gone. 'In the 1990s and early 2000s there was some justification for an incrementalist strategy', writes Clive Hamilton, author of *Requiem for a Species: Why we resist the truth about climate change*. 'But climate science now shows that the situation has become so urgent, and the forecasts so dire, that only radical social and economic transformation will give us a chance of avoiding dramatic and irreversible changes to the global climate.'

* * *

Of course, it is not as if people are unaware of the changes in our climate or other societal risks. Unfortunately, as I will explore in the next section, being relentlessly warned about these threats is not motivating most of us to change. This is not a book exposing the ills of tourism. That has been done superbly by the likes of Leo Hickman in *Last Call* and Elizabeth Becker in *Overbooked*.

This is a book about the best of tourism. It is not filled with terrible statistics but inspiring stories. Sometimes the people behind these stories win awards, and occasionally they get written about. But they are mostly seen as outliers, presented as exceptions. In this book I want to imagine what our industry might look like if we instead modelled it on the approaches and actions of these in-novators and pioneers. Because, as Steve Howard, the chief sustainability officer for IKEA, writes of his own company's efforts to reinvent its business model: 'Incrementalism doesn't light people up. It is radical change that excites.'[8]

---

[7] David Harrison and Richard Sharpley (eds) (2017), *Mass Tourism in a Small World*, p. 66.
[8] https://www.businessgreen.com/bg/interview/2392561/ikea-green-business-incrementalism-excites-no-one (accessed 4 August 2017).

How can tourism excite people towards transformative change?

Some refer to Sustainable Tourism. Others prefer Responsible Tourism. Along with Ecotourism, these three are the best known and most used terms. However, you'll also find Geotourism, Green Tourism, Fair Trade Tourism, Pro-Poor Tourism, Conscious Tourism, and more.

We have the International Ecotourism Society. The US-based Sustainable Travel International. The long-running holiday booking website Responsibletravel.com. Certification of hotels and tour companies is done in Australia by Ecotourism Australia; by Fair Trade Tourism in South Africa (along with Madagascar and Mozambique); by Green Tourism in the UK (who also take the reins in three regions in Canada, two in Italy and in Zimbabwe). And the body that is trying to tidy all this up is called the Global Sustainable Tourism Council.

At first glance they seem to have similar objectives. Fair Trade Tourism says it is 'defined by fair wages and working conditions, fair purchasing and operations, equitable distribution of benefits and respect for human rights, culture and the environment'.[9] Sustainable Travel International declares its mission to be 'Improving lives and protecting places through travel and tourism'. Meanwhile, the Cape Town Declaration on Responsible Tourism calls on the industry 'to take responsibility for achieving sustainable tourism, and to create better places for people to live in and for people to visit'.

Then again, while the UN declared 2017 to be the International Year of Sustainable Tourism for Development, responsibletravel.com says that because of the climate impacts of aviation, 'one expression we never use is "sustainable tourism"'. It can all get rather confusing, especially for the tourist looking to switch off for a few days and weeks and forget about their daily worries.

* * *

'Travel is double free time: it frees people from work and from home', wrote Jost Krippendorf in *The Holiday Makers*[10], one of the first books to examine the environmental and social impacts of the then emerging mass tourism industry. By contrast, people associate demands to act more responsibly and sustainability with imposing restrictions on our freedoms, and placing limits on our behaviour. Campaigns to drink alcohol responsibly really mean drink less. Concepts such as responsible tourism or sustainable tourism are impeded by simultaneously trying to promote freedom and impose restrictions on it. 'The people who are most concerned about the inhabitants of other countries are often those who have travelled widely', writes environmentalist George Monbiot.

---

[9] http://www.fairtrade.travel/Home/ (accessed 30 May 2017).
[10] Jost Krippendorf (1987) *The Holiday Makers*, p. 27.

Much of the global justice movement consists of people – like me – whose politics were forged by their experiences abroad. While it is easy for us to pour scorn on the drivers of sports utility vehicles, whose politics generally differ from ours, it is rather harder to contemplate a world in which our own freedoms are curtailed, especially the freedoms that shaped us.

In 2014 the founder of the Climate Outreach and Information Network George Marshall published *Don't Even Think about It – Why our brains are hardwired to ignore climate change*, a book exploring why, despite overwhelming scientific evidence, the vast majority of us act as if climate change does not exist. 'Everything we see and hear about climate change triggers frames', writes Marshall, 'responsibility, resistance, freedom, science, rights, pollution, consumption, waste – all are frames with their own associations.'[11]

Such frames, he explains, result in the sort of confused situations where 'Republicans were five times more willing to pay a two per cent climate change surcharge on an airline ticket when it was described as a carbon offset than when it was called a carbon tax'. Or where in an effort to reduce theft by visitors, officials at Arizona Petrified Forest National Park put up a sign stating: 'Your heritage is being vandalized every day by theft losses of petrified wood of 14 tons a year, mostly a small piece at a time'. Yet rates of theft increased after the sign was erected, because, explains Marshall, 'although the sign attempted to communicate the undesirability of theft, what it actually communicated far more powerfully was that stealing a small amount of wood was a perfectly normal activity'.[12]

Our efforts to promote sustainable or responsible tourism suffer because the way sustainability is commonly framed contradicts the way tourism is perceived. Having enjoyed hundreds of the world's best ventures labelled as responsible/sustainable/eco/fair tourism across the planet, I know they offer me the best experiences out there. If my friends ask for recommendations, these are what I share. Yet because the many positives that I believe such forms of tourism create – better experiences, warmer welcomes, tastier food, etc. – are not immediately associated in most people's imaginations with the concepts of sustainability and responsibility, I don't use such labels to promote them.

'It is unfortunate that the most common compounds of all, *high carbon* and *low carbon*, are used to differentiate lifestyles, economies, and technologies', writes Marshall.

> 'High' is a universal frame for status and power. We say high-class, high-end, high quality, high achievement. 'Low' is a universal frame for inferiority and social failure. No matter how much you try to bend it, 'high carbon living' sounds intuitively like having champagne in a penthouse and 'low carbon living' sounds like drinking cold tea in a dank basement.

---

[11] George Marshall (2014) *Don't Even Think about It*, p. 109.
[12] George Marshall (2014) *Don't Even Think about It*, p. 30.

Why is 'transformative' different?

In the last year or so, there has been a marked increase in the use of various forms of the word 'transformation' to describe and promote certain types of tourism. The UNWTO released a report in 2016 called *Transformative Tourism for Our Sustainable Future*.[13] Featuring case studies from around the world, it was edited by Irena Ateljevic, a researcher leading a team who in 2018 will conclude a four-year project 'TRANS-TOURISM: An integrated approach for the study of transformative role of tourism in the 21st century', funded by the Croatian Science Foundation. According to Ateljevic, her research has found that

> increasingly more and more people are seeing their holidays as the one time when they can reflect on life and imagine what alternatives there might be. They are too busy working in their daily lives to do otherwise so they use their time away from work to actively seek out places and experiences that provide an opportunity for transformation.[14]

An article in *Vogue* magazine in January 2017 was headlined 'Why "transformative travel" will be the travel trend of 2017'.[15] It described the trend as 'travel motivated and defined by a shift in perspective, self-reflection and development, and a deeper communion with nature and culture'. The luxury travel event Pure has an award category for 'Transformative Travel'. There's also an organization in America called the Transformational Travel Council, which offers consultancy to those in the industry looking to tap into the trend by 'scrapping the typical itinerary to consciously design experiences that will transform your life'.[16]

Meanwhile, in March 2017 at ITB Berlin, the world's largest travel fair, a group representing NGOs, civil society groups and academia launched The Berlin Declaration on Transforming Tourism. Unlike the examples mentioned above, however, their declaration was not concerned with promoting a form of tourism that focuses on deeper personal enrichment for the visitor. Instead, their motivation for using the word 'Transform' was the same as that of the United Nations. In 2015, the UN adopted the 17 Sustainable Development Goals, focusing on issues such as ending poverty and hunger, improving health and education, making cities more sustainable, addressing climate change, and protecting oceans and forests. The whole thing is collectively known as *Transforming Our World: the 2030 Agenda for Sustainable Development*. 'As tourism experts and practitioners, we are concerned that the current dominant tourism model is not able to

---

[13] http://affiliatemembers.unwto.org/content/am-reports-volume-13-transformative-tourism-our-sustainable-future (accessed 30 May 2017).
[14] Personal communication, 15 August 2017.
[15] http://www.vogue.com/article/transformative-travel-trend-2017 (accessed 30 May 2017).
[16] http://www.transformational.travel/about-tt/ (accessed 24 June 2017).

support the necessary transformation of our world envisaged by the 2030 Agenda', states the Berlin Declaration. 'On the contrary, in too many cases it is exploiting people, harming communities, violating human rights and degrading the environment. Transforming our world is not possible without transforming tourism.'

This book explores how to weave together both interpretations. What model should tourism follow to positively transform people's lives and the environment? And how should we communicate this to tourists looking for transformative experiences?

However, I am not suggesting part of the answer is more use of the phrase 'transformative tourism'. One of the reasons we have so many terms now is because earlier terms got adopted, then co-opted and then rejected.

Ecotourism came first. And it is still the term that gets by far the most results on a search engine. But popularity came at the price of authority. Any accommodation establishment in natural surroundings can call itself an eco-lodge. Often they are doing little to benefit the environment they operate in. I have seen the same happen to the word 'heritage' in the UNESCO World Heritage site at Georgetown, Malaysia, where coffeeshops and cafes use the word in their names despite only having just launched.

And so it goes on. Earlier critics of the term ecotourism are often just as divided about the words sustainable, responsible, green and more. It follows that the word transformation is as open to misuse.

The underlying concept it defines remains the same, however, and this is what interests me. Transformation is defined by the dictionary as 'a sudden, dramatic change' or 'metamorphosis'. This focus on the urgency and scale of change required adds an important dimension to the more common terms, responsible and sustainable. Responsible focuses on behaviour, connecting us to the impacts of our actions and our responsibility for them, and ensures that these actions comply with a set of ethical guidelines. Sustainable looks more at the result of such actions, and implies that the existence and operation of a product, service or activity can be sustained by our environment. These are important concepts, and I am not looking to supplant them. However, neither necessarily imply any change to the world around them, or the person engaging in the behaviour. Often their aim is for things to be left as they were.

Transformation differs because it is dynamic – it demands movement, change and agency. It defines a process designed to interact with and make positive change, on an individual and/or on the world. As the issues around us become more urgent, and as it becomes apparent that our current incrementalist approaches are insufficient, then this additional concept is necessary.

Tourism also demands change and movement. We go on holiday for a change of scene. For some it is enough just for their skin to become a little more tanned, while others seek life-changing experiences. We don't need to develop a 'transformative tourism' certification scheme. We just need to ensure the transformations tourism causes are as positive as possible.

Transformation also moves beyond the common perception that the goal of environmentally responsible tourism should be to tread as lightly as possible, reducing our damaging impacts towards a goal often defined as 'Leave no trace'. There are times when this 'take only pictures, leave only footsteps' approach is exactly the right one – when camping or in fragile natural environments, for example. Acting according to such principles helps us to become much more aware of the resources we take for granted. Beyond that, however, the concept of 'Leave no trace' positions humanity as a threatening force and attempts to minimize and remove the damage resulting from our presence. It risks further separating us from the nature we live in and are part of. Like incrementalism, it lacks the power to motivate greater change. Transformation offers us the chance of an active regenerative role.

What does transformation mean for tourism?

Just as many people think taking a responsible holiday sounds less fun, so many companies see creating a sustainable or responsible product or experience as being about doing it while causing less harm. Reduce your emissions. Use fewer resources. Create less waste.

Such an approach creates conflicts for industry. Presented this way, acting more sustainably is framed as an external cost that goes against a company's core remit to deliver maximum profit to its stakeholders. It is a compromise brought about by regulation or other pressures. That's why it is introduced incrementally.

Essentially, this is a linear approach that sees all processes as starting, creating something, making some waste along the way, then tidying up or reducing that waste on the path to an end goal. Incrementally improving this approach does not question the approach itself. It does not ask whether an economic system that meant municipalities in the USA spent US$5 billion to dispose of waste in 2015 could be better designed so the inherent value and energy in the materials we throw away can be captured. It assumes that the model is basically sound, but maybe needs a bit of refining.

This linear approach is not the way nature works. 'Nature does not know the concept of waste; the only species capable of making something no one desires is the human species',[17] writes Gunther Pauli, founder of the environmental cleaning product company Ecover and the Zero Emissions Resource Institute, one of a growing number of organizations exploring how modelling the way business, industry and society operate on natural processes might work.

'Today's linear "take, make, dispose" economic model relies on large quantities of cheap, easily accessible materials and energy, and is a model that

---

[17] http://www.zeri.org/ZERI/Future_Vision.html (accessed 1 June 2017).

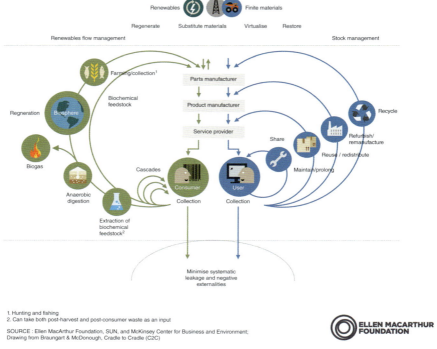

Fig. 1.2. How the circular economy's regenerative design works. (Courtesy of Ellen MacArthur Foundation.)

is reaching its physical limits',[18] explains the Ellen MacArthur Foundation, which collaborates with business and civil society to develop more circular ways of working. On the other hand: 'A circular economy is restorative and regenerative by design, and aims to keep products, components, and materials at their highest utility and value at all times.'

Dame Ellen MacArthur first came to fame aged 28, when she achieved what was then the fastest single-handed circumnavigation of the globe, sailing more than 26,000 miles in just over 71 days. In an interview with McKinsey she explained how she came to launch her foundation:

> When you set off around the world, you take with you everything that you need for your survival. So for three, three and a half months, you're on a boat with everything that you have. You know that you only have so much food, you only have so much diesel, and you become incredibly connected to those resources that you use. And as you watch those resources go down, you realise just what 'finite' means, because in the Southern Ocean, you're 2,500 miles away from the nearest town. There is no more, you can't stop and collect more. I'd never made that translation to anything other than

---

[18] https://www.ellenmacarthurfoundation.org/circular-economy/overview/concept (accessed 1 June 2017).

sailing, but suddenly I realised our global economy is no different. It's powered on resources which are ultimately finite. And I suddenly realised that there was a much greater challenge out there than sailing around the world, which was, in fact, trying to find a global economy that could function in the long term.[19]

The potential is huge. A study of seven European countries has found that shifting to a circular economy would see each nation's greenhouse-gas emissions cut by up to 70% while growing their workforce by about 4%. According to McKinsey, new circular ways of working could boost the world's economy by US$1 trillion by 2025 and create 100,000 new jobs within the next five years. In 2016, the Netherlands government presented a vision for the country to adopt a fully circular economy by 2050.

The Ellen MacArthur Foundation now has 100 or more major corporations and organizations listed as being members of its 'Circular Economy 100', including the likes of Apple, Cisco, Coca-Cola, eBay, Google, IKEA and many more household names. When I went through the list on 1 September 2017, however, there was not a single tourism company, and from the travel sector the only representative was Schipol Airport.

I find this disconnect strange. Record-breaking it may have been, but her journey was in essence an extreme version of what we all do when we go on holiday. Tourism is defined in many ways, but one key constant is that it is a circular trip. We pack our bags and head off somewhere else. And eventually we end up back at home. If your journey ends where you travel to, most people would consider you a migrant, not a tourist.

The trips we buy do more than just give us a tan and some memories. There are the emissions from our journeys and from our stay. The impact our contact with the people we visit has, both on us and them. Where our money ends up and who and what it supports (or doesn't) as a result. Some of these might be factored into the costs we pay, but most, especially the hidden or indirect ones, are not.

These hidden, indirect, impacts – both social and environmental – are known as externalities. They can be positive, such as when a bee producing honey for a beekeeper flies off and pollinates the fields of nearby farmers. More often they are negative. 'The hotel owner does not count the emissions generated by guests and most source countries don't either', writes Anna Pollock, founder of Conscious Travel, an initiative that explores more deeply than any other the theoretical and philosophical framework for a circular, regenerative travel industry.

For example, the carbon associated with international trips made by Britons when travelling overseas does not form part of the UK's carbon budget. When

---

[19] http://www.mckinsey.com/business-functions/sustainability-and-resource-productivity/our-insights/navigating-the-circular-economy-a-conversation-with-dame-ellen-macarthur (accessed 1 June 2017).

boring into an underground aquifer to access fresh water, does the owner of the theme park check that the farmer miles up the road still has sufficient pressure to irrigate the lettuce being delivered to hotels each morning? Perhaps we ensure that the trash is sorted into bins and removed by the council but have we seen the local landfill site and how well it is managed and staffed and whether toxins are leaching into the groundwater?[20]

Applying the principles of the circular economy to tourism means asking how we either redesign our systems to avoid causing these externalities, or rethink them so they can be factored productively back in. Furthermore, because the industry employs so many people and provides holiday encounters for even more, there is an opportunity for it to feed positively back into the next stages in development of the circular economy, which has so far been predominantly focused on issues around materials and waste. Tourism can be a leader in adding a much-needed social dimension.

As Alexandre Lemille, a circular economy expert working to add a social persepctive to current models, writes:

> These externalities also exist at societal levels in our unequal-unable-inaccessible model: inequality, unemployment, fictitious capital (debt) creating poverty so that wealth could be built for others, people living with disability seen as less 'performing', and so on. How about taking this opportunity to also see poverty as the result of a wrongly designed system? How about claiming that – like waste – poverty is an externality of our current model? Like waste, shouldn't it be designed out too?[21]

How can the sharing economy support transformation?

Although these ideas are little talked about in tourism, the sharing economy, especially in the guise of Airbnb and similar home-sharing sites, is well known. In principle, the sharing economy is part of the circular economy, one which looks to reduce waste by optimizing the use of assets – such as spare rooms or empty flats in the case of Airbnb.

Airbnb both illustrates the transformative potential of the sharing economy and the challenges that come with it. It shows how fast change can happen and how it can radically change both an industry and how individuals interact, and how this can capture the minds of millions of travellers. Airbnb only started in 2008. It now makes available more rooms than any other accommodation provider in the world. And it does all this through a model that relies on people trusting total strangers to stay in their most valuable and loved possession, often while they are not there.

---

[20] Anna Pollock (2016) *Social Entrepreneurship and Tourism: Setting the Stage*, p. 80.
[21] http://www.huffingtonpost.com/alexandre-lemille/circular-economy-20_b_9376488.html (accessed 20 August 2017).

Airbnb is also increasingly being criticized for the negative externalities resulting from its rapid growth, such as exacerbating overtourism in cities through adding considerably to the number of potential places people can stay; causing rent prices to increase, thus costing residents out of the most desirable parts of their own cities; altering the social fabric of residential neighbourhoods; and not paying sufficient tax revenue to municipal administrations.

Airbnb and the technologies it utilizes are not going away soon. Regulation is necessary, yet regulation has not developed as fast as these new business models. 'The sharing economy is creating negative externalities that traditional regulation is often ill-equipped to address', writes Urs Gasser, Executive Director at Harvard's Berkman Center for Internet & Society, in a report exploring what effective regulation might look like.

> Short-term rentals, like Airbnb, can lead to increased noise and foot traffic in apartment buildings or quiet neighborhoods. Regulations like zoning laws are effective at keeping big hotels out of residential neighborhoods, but they frequently have little to say about renting out an apartment or house for a week or two.[22]

As Gasser's report makes clear, these rapidly developing ways of doing business are going to need new forms of regulation to ensure they maximize benefits to all they affect, while addressing whatever new externalities result.

While Airbnb and Uber utilize the structures of the sharing economy to make very profitable businesses, there are also sharing platforms where social impact is the priority. There's Bewelcome, which describes itself as the 'first non-profit and open source based travel and hospitality exchange'. Trustroots, which says it is 'being built by a small team of activists who felt that the world of sharing is being taken over by corporations trying to monetize people's willingness to help each other'. And the developers behind the Fairbnb.coop project say they are developing a valid alternative to commercial platforms so as to answer two questions:

> What if, in the world of short-term accommodation rentals, guests, hosts and neighbours could collectively decide together with municipalities how to make the rental process fairer, more sustainable and more rewarding for the whole community? What if the platform's profits were not an end in themselves but were invested back into the communities where the platform operates?

Can we do more than reduce our impact on climate change?

Tourism's biggest externality is its carbon emissions, and their impact on climate change. In this book, I have largely based my approach to dealing with this on the work of Project Drawdown, which brings together many

---

[22] http://institute.swissre.com/research/risk_dialogue/magazine/Digital_Economy/ sharing_economy_disruptive_effects.html (accessed 4 August 2017).

of the world's most eminent climate scientists and has been appointed to collaborate on future research with the Commonwealth Secretariat, which has committed to integrating Drawdown's work into the economic and ecological portfolios of its 52 countries, representing almost one-third of humanity. In 2016, founder Paul Hawken published a synthesis of its work, titled *Drawdown – The Most Comprehensive Plan Ever Proposed to Reverse Global Warming*. Like the circular economy, the book is based on the premise that we need to rethink industry and society in such a way that works with nature rather than against it. And it starts from the startling premise that our approach to addressing climate change is wrong.

At school, we all learned that plants grow by taking in carbon dioxide through the process of photosynthesis. Nature does not see carbon dioxide as an enemy, something to be beaten. It is a building block of life. 'Anthropogenic greenhouse gases in the atmosphere make airborne carbon a material in the wrong place, at the wrong dose and wrong duration', writes circular economy pioneer, Michael Braungart. 'It is we who have made carbon a toxin – like lead in our drinking water. In the right place, carbon is a resource and tool.'[23]

Just as we need to re-evaluate how we relate to carbon, so we need to remember that

> Climate changes because it always has and will, and variations of climate produce everything from seasons to evolution. The goal is to come into alignment with the impact we are having on the climate by addressing the human causes of global warming and bringing carbon back home.[24]

Bringing carbon back home. These last four words are central to the work of Project Drawdown, and its first book, which sets out, by comparing their impact and measuring their cost, what are the hundred most powerful things we can do to reverse global warming by drawing down carbon from the atmosphere and returning it to the earth. 'Addressing, slowing, or arresting emissions is necessary, but insufficient', writes Hawken.

> If you are travelling down the wrong road, you are still on the wrong road if you slow down. The only goal that makes sense for humanity is to reverse global warming, and if parents, scientists, young people, leaders, and we citizens do not name the goal, there is little chance that it will be achieved.[25]

The wood. And the trees.

The dream of going on holiday captures our imagination. It takes us out of our daily routines and shows us visions of other places and realities, of other

[23] https://www.environmentalleader.com/2016/11/the-war-on-carbon-is-over/ (accessed 30 July 2017).
[24] Paul Hawken (2017) *Drawdown*, p. 111.
[25] Paul Hawken (2017) *Drawdown*, p. 111.

ways of living. Nothing else gives us the same chance to experiment with being someone else, somewhere else. As the environmental writer (and one of Project Drawdown's advisory board) Bill McKibben says, this 'may be the most useful thing about travel'.[26]

Climate change, and our collective response to it, will to a large part define the future of the majority of people currently alive, and of all of their children and grandchildren. We need to create the tools and systems to cope with already rising temperatures while reducing the carbon dioxide emissions we cause as much as possible and drawing them back down into balance with the earth's natural systems. We need to do this in such a way that doesn't exacerbate poverty and forced migration, or jeopardize our food security and health. And because this demands we redesign the industrial processes that cause these emissions, we will need to rethink our relationship to productivity and work.

There are other issues. Environmentally, we need to protect and restore biodiversity and tackle pollution. Socially, we have to rebuild fractured societies, address widening inequalities, and preserve vulnerable cultures and heritage. And we need to learn how all of these are inextricably linked. Environmental degradation affects the poorest members of our societies the most. Economic inequalities and mental health are exacerbated by limited access to nature.

The approaches that underpin the circular economy and *Drawdown* offer realistic solutions to all these challenges. For most people, however, they remain obscure and little understood abstractions. By embracing them as the model for development, tourism can make them real, and help people discover and experience their potential through enjoying hotels, tours and places that follow these circular, inclusive, regenerative principles. Properly regulated, tourism designed and operated this way would ensure that societies and environments benefit from its presence, which could go a long way to addressing the increasing resistance to the industry in those places most threatened by its excesses. And it can do all this when we are at our most relaxed and open, and by helping us share pleasure and discovery together. Warning people of the risks of our current way of living has failed to produce change. Might giving us the opportunity to experience new ways have more chance of success?

That's the concept. The rest of this book explores what it might look like.

---

[26] www.travelandleisure.com/articles/global-warming-and-the-travelers-world (accessed 27 October 2017).

The Transformative Hotel

The future is for hoteliers to build lodging establishments that are not only energy-efficient and environmentally-friendly, but inspired by and adaptable to natural habitats. Imagine a hotel that breathes; a hotel that generates power and cools itself using the wind, absorbs sunlight for energy, collects and recycles rainwater from underground pools, and is covered with a landscaped roof. These lodging establishments modeled after nature are our aspiration (and the future).

Lorraine Francis
Director, Sustainable Hospitality Committee
Hospitality Industry Network

The visionary industrialist

Let's start on the ground floor. Or any other floor. In 1973, Ray C. Anderson founded industrial carpet company Interface with what then seemed a crazy innovation – to cut rolls of carpets into square tiles. Twenty-one years later, the company was the world's largest producer of the now commonplace modular carpet, with manufacturing on four continents and sales in more than 110 countries. But that year, tasked to prepare a speech on his company's environmental strategy, Anderson, who at the time drove a Bentley and in no way considered himself an environmentalist, felt unprepared.

Seeking ideas, he turned to an earlier book by *Drawdown* editor Paul Hawken, *The Ecology of Commerce*. 'I read it and it changed my life', said Anderson. 'It was an epiphany. I wasn't halfway through it before the vision I sought became clear, along with a powerful sense of urgency to do something. Hawken's message was a spear in my chest that remains to this day.'

Anderson set about radically realigning the way his company worked. Shocking shareholders and much of his staff, he committed Interface's vision to be

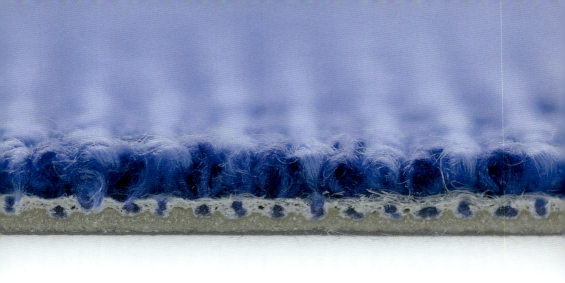

Fig. 2.1. Proof Positive tiles turn your floor into a carbon sink. (Courtesy of Interface.)

the first company that, by its deeds, shows the entire industrial world what sustainability is in all its dimensions: people, process, product, place, and profits – by 2020 – and by doing so we will become restorative through the power of influence.

Why am I talking about carpets? First, because Interface's story is a perfect example of how just about any company, in any field, can radically transform the way it does business and become more successful as a result. And secondly, because hotels are hubs at the centre of complex networks and supply chains. They are filled with as much variety of products and furnishing as any house or office in the world. Every product decision has an impact, every choice is an opportunity to transform.

Ray Anderson died in 2011. But Interface has continued his vision, and is now a billion-dollar business. The company has reduced water intake by 87%. Greenhouse gas emissions at its manufacturing sites are down 92%. And in 2017 it released a prototype tile known as Proof Positive, another first-of-its-kind in the surprisingly radical world of modular carpet tiles.

Although plants absorb carbon from the atmosphere, they re-release it as they decompose. Interface has therefore created a tile from plant-based materials, thus storing that carbon for at least a generation. When the tile's carpet is worn out, Interface takes it and processes it into a new tile. This means the carbon stays in a closed loop as opposed to being released into the atmosphere.

Proof Positive epitomizes the principles of Project Drawdown in the way Interface now describes its corporate mission as 'Climate Take Back'. Moving beyond efforts to slow or reduce global warming, they are instead exploring ways to reverse it through an approach to business that should be how the tourism industry reimagines its development. It's based on the following four tenets:

1. Live Zero – Do business in ways that give back whatever is taken from the Earth.
2. Love Carbon – Stop seeing carbon as the enemy, and start using it as a resource.
3. Let Nature Cool – Support our biosphere's ability to regulate the climate.
4. Lead Industrial Re-revolution – Transform industry into a force for climate progress.[1]

This is what you can do when you rethink a carpet. Just imagine what we can do if we rethink an entire hotel.

Design waste out of your system

Waste isn't usually the first thing people think of; in fact, we tend to think about it last. We use a product, and then we look around for the right way to dispose of it.

I am starting with waste because it exemplifies the transformation in approach that this book is about. Like Ray Anderson and Interface, it's time to stop thinking about waste at the end, and see acting this way as a wasted opportunity. Instead, every product decision, every design choice, every manufacturing process, should be guided by questions like: what are the external consequences of my purchasing decisions that I might be ignoring? What will happen to this product at the end of its life? What can I do with all the materials left over through production? Can I use them another way or return them into the system?

The Belgian hotel chain Martin's won a European Eco-Management and Audit Scheme award in 2017 for its circular economy approach to its supply chain. Hotel floors are covered with carpet tiles supplied by Desso, who work in similar ways to Interface. Using their tiles, only the damaged pieces are replaced instead of the entire carpet, and all products are designed to be recyclable to allow the reuse of materials in new, superior-quality products.

Likewise, everything from computers and coffee machines, fitness equipment to company cars, are leased, lowering the total cost of ownership by enabling, at the end of leasing, either reuse or buy-back/resale, recycling or donation.[2] This leasing model, known as Product as Service, 'can allow closer relations with the customer, enhanced product development from closer feedback loops, provide greater business value to both parties and improve customer satisfaction', according to Cambridge University's

---

[1] http://www.interface.com/US/en-US/campaign/climate-take-back/Four-Pillars-en_US (accessed 27 October 2017).
[2] https://www.travindy.com/2017/05/martins-hotels-circular-economy-supply-chain/ (accessed 31 May 2017).

Circular Economy Toolkit.[3] An increasing range of products are available this way – for example, the Swiss company Elite leases eco-certified bedding such as mattresses, duvets, sheets and pillows to hotels.

Because a hotel's supply chain is so extensive, there are countless opportunities for adopting a circular economy approach. And each one not only offers a better way of producing something, it provides an opportunity for that choice to tell a story about your company.

There are clothing manufacturers working to repurpose old materials into new clothes that could be used for staff uniforms or branded products sold to guests. UK company Vivobarefoot is making shoes out of biomass harvested from ponds and lakes, particularly those at risk from algal overload. Parley for the Oceans has been working with Adidas to create footwear using waste plastic collected from the oceans. A seafront hotel could clean up its beach, and finance and promote the operation by selling clothing in the hotel made from the waste.

At W Hotels, they worked with Ekocycle to repurpose old cola bottles (read the first four letters of Ekocycle backwards) into new bed sheets. Each king-size Ekocycle sheet contains around 31 recycled 600-ml plastic bottles. Meanwhile, Marriott is partnering with a UK social enterprise called SleepingBags[4] to repurpose hotel bed linen that has reached the end of its life back into items that can be used in guest rooms – such as bathrobes, tote bags and slippers.

In Ahmedabad, in the India state of Gujarat, ReMaterials has designed a roofing product called ModRoof, with tiles made of waste cardboard, pressed together with coconut fibre and non-toxic bonding agents, and covered in a non-toxic waterproof coating. They are waterproof, fireproof and, like Interface's tiles, can be disassembled piece by piece and moved or replaced. It is currently prototyping embedding solar cells in them too. According to the Ellen MacArthur Foundation, circular initiatives like this could generate an additional US$624 billion for India by 2050.

At the Modez design hotel in the Netherlands, the beds and mattresses in its 20 rooms were designed by Dutch firm Auping, the first bed manufacturer in the world to be awarded Cradle to Cradle silver certification, as more than 50% of the materials in their beds have been or can be reused. Developed first by the designers Michael Braungart and William McDonough, Cradle to Cradle[5] is a regenerative design approach which models human industry on nature's processes by viewing materials as nutrients circulating in healthy, safe metabolisms. There are also Cradle to Cradle products available for flooring, rugs, upholstery, countertops, towels, blankets, pillows, window shades, wall and floor tiles and paint. Even toilet paper.

---

[3] http://circulareconomytoolkit.org/products-as-a-service.html (accessed 9 August 2017).
[4] http://www.sleepingbags.me (accessed 1 June 2017).
[5] http://www.c2ccertified.org (accessed 1 June 2017).

The zero waste hotel

> Zero Waste means designing and managing products and processes to reduce
> the volume and toxicity of waste and materials, conserve and recover all
> resources, and not burn or bury them. Implementing Zero Waste will eliminate
> all discharges to land, water, or air that may be a threat to planetary, human,
> animal or plant health.[6]

The Four Seasons in Austin set a zero waste goal in 2013, which meant 'effectively limiting the property to six square feet of uncompacted trash daily'.
By January 2014 the hotel was designated as zero waste following an audit
that found it had successfully diverted 263 tons of waste through recycling
and 262 tons through compost, decreasing its environmental waste foot-
print by a factor of nine in little over a year. While continuing its efforts to
recover even more waste, the hotel is also now creating a Zero Waste Case
Study and Guide designed to help Austin and other local businesses become
zero waste. Adopting an open source approach to sharing the knowledge
gained through such initiatives is essential if we are to stop wasting time
reinventing the wheel and rather accelerate the shift towards a more collaborative, regenerative society.

At the other end of the budgetary scale, the Fair and Square Hostel in
Belgrade combines on-site recycling facilities with the extensive use of upcycled materials in its fixtures and fittings[7], from scrap metal to hand-made
tables made from wood panels. In so doing it moves beyond the approach of
reducing one's waste to as near zero as possible, and begins to ask of every
material used, how can we take this out of the waste stream and return it
to use?

Luxury Maldives hotel Soneva Fushi set up an Eco Centro Waste to
Wealth centre, designed using permaculture principles. Despite being located on an island atoll with no municipal waste facilities, the hotel now
recycles 81% of its solid waste.[8] Glass is crushed and used as a replacement
for sand in concrete making and in 2013 Soneva Fushi also took in over 4.5
tonnes of plastic bottles and metal cans from the surrounding islands, which
it compacted for recycling. Just as The Four Seasons Austin has looked to
circulate its knowledge as widely as possible, so Soneva's support for its
community reminds us that we should also look to use the solutions we develop more widely than just in our own core business.

At Soneva, food waste is composted using a forced aeration composting
system, producing compost that fertilizes 3000 m^2 of herb and vegetable

---

[6] https://www.zerowasteeurope.eu/about/principles-zw-europe/ (accessed 31 May 2017).
[7] http://inhabitat.com/5-star-rated-fair-and-square-hostel-in-belgrade-combines-
upcycling-renewable-energy-and-on-site-waste-recycling/ (accessed 31 May 2017).
[8] http://www.greenhotelier.org/our-themes/waste/soneva-fushi-recycles-81-of-solid-
waste/ (accessed 31 May 2017).

Fig. 2.2. Glass bottles are reused in the bathroom walls at Ecuador's Black Sheep Inn.

gardens, on what would otherwise be sandy and salty soil unsuitable for growing crops, and supplying the kitchen with 9000 kg of organic fresh produce per year, which equates to 100% of herbs and 30% of salads consumed.

Biochar is made by slowly baking biomass waste in the near or total absence of oxygen, causing the gas and oil to separate from carbon-rich solids. The hotel has built biochar ovens that convert woody waste to charcoal for barbeques and the pizza oven, and biochar for the soil. It is now self-reliant in charcoal, saving US$24,000 and further reducing its carbon footprint.

According to Project Drawdown, we could use biochar to sequester billions of tons of carbon dioxide every year.[9]

The Black Sheep Inn in Ecuador has been zero waste for many years, reducing its environmental impact by buying in bulk and avoiding non-recyclable packaging, reusing paper, cardboard, glass bottles, large plastic containers, kitchen scraps, and water and human waste onsite thanks to compost toilets. Guests heading out for a hike are offered packed lunches in unbleached brown paper. The inn does not sell bottled water, but allows guests to fill

---

[9] http://www.drawdown.org/solutions/food/biochar (accessed 9 August 2017).

their bottles with ozone-purified water for free. Glass bottles are reused in the walls of the saunas and showers. Newspapers are mulched into the garden. Food scraps are composted or fed to animals.

Like Soneva, the inn has set up a recycling centre that not only meets its needs but also services the nearby village, which previously had no recycling facilities. As the inn's website explains:

> Trash used to be swept weekly in the canyon in front of the local school. Now trash is separated into cardboard, hard plastic, soft plastic, paper, metal and organic. Recyclables are sold and profits go directly to the people who sort the waste. Organic waste has been composted and used to fertilize a public central park in the village.[10]

Thanks to the hotel, it means that where previously the village's waste despoiled the landscape, now over 50% is composted, 30% separated and sold to local recyclers and just 20% goes into a small landfill.

Black Sheep Inn has received huge amounts of press for its efforts, winning the Green Hotelier Award 2015 as the Best in the Americas, been rated Platinum by TripAdvisor Green Leaders and was included in the World's Best Hotels by National Geographic Traveler. What started with waste management has led to a supportive community, a hotel full of guests and a shelf loaded with awards.

Can a hotel reduce global warming?

According to 2017 research from Greenview, commissioned by the International Tourism Partnership, the global hotel sector needs to reduce its absolute emissions by 90% by 2030. First off, therefore, any hotel needs to measure and be transparent about its impacts, and what any reductions really mean. For example, a hotel chain may report that it has reduced its emissions by 20% per year over the past five years. But this top line figure can mean various things, depending on the detail.

It can mean that whereas before it produced a total of – say – 100 tonnes of climate-altering emissions, it now produces 80 tonnes. Alternatively, it might mean that it has made its individual hotels more efficient by 20%, so that where each hotel was responsible for 10 tonnes of emissions before, it is now responsible for 8 tonnes. This is of course an improvement. If the hotel chain didn't expand its operations over that time, then a chain with ten hotels will indeed have cut its emissions to 80 tonnes.

However, if this ten-hotel chain has also built four new hotels in the last year, then the chain will have produced 14×8 tonnes of emissions = 112 tonnes. So what can be presented as a 20% reduction, since each hotel is 20% more efficient, is also a 12% increase in its total climate impact.

---

[10] http://blacksheepinn.com/ecological/community.php#recycling (accessed 31 May 2017).

On the other hand, suppose the hotel chain buys four already existing hotels, which for the sake of argument also produce 10 tonnes of emissions. It also makes them 20% more efficient. The total emissions from its chain will have risen, because it now owns more hotels. However, the total climate impact of the 14 buildings, regardless of who owns them, has gone down.

There is a fourth scenario. Having reduced its emissions by 20%, the hotel chain then buys into a carbon offset scheme that says it will offset a further 50% of its emissions. As a result, the hotel chain says that it has reduced its net carbon emissions by 70%. In reality though, it has paid for someone else to do so, or paid for a service to absorb or produce less carbon somewhere else in the world.

What role do carbon offsets offer towards transformation?

Offsetting epitomizes the contradiction and confusion at the heart of tourism's sustainability efforts, with many hotels, tour companies and airlines supporting it as part of their approach to addressing their impact on climate change. Meanwhile, critics reject offsetting as a damaging distraction that confers a licence to carry on business as usual, while others change.

This has resulted in an extremely confusing situation, where among companies who claim to offer responsible or sustainable tourism, some offer links to sites offering to offset individual tourists' emissions, some factor them into the costs they charge tourists, some explicitly state that they reject them, and some make no mention of them at all.

If we are to find a correct answer, or at least not support a wrong one, then the following questions need discussing by the industry urgently, and far more openly than it currently does. Only then can we provide clarity to tourists.

What impact do offsets have on a company's carbon emissions?

None. Say my hotel (or flight, or other activity) emits 1 tonne of carbon dioxide, so I buy 1 tonne of offsets. These offsets supply families currently using coal or oil-powered stoves with solar-powered ones. A year later, thanks to them no longer using these old stoves, their contribution of CO_2 into the environment is 1 tonne less than it would have been. It is they, or at least their cooking, which now emits no (or less) carbon, since it is their emissions that have gone down. My hotel is still emitting 1 tonne of CO_2.

What impacts do offsets have on global warming?

Variable, although potentially good. Some offsets provide finance to schemes that replace polluting technologies with clean ones, for example supplying people with solar-powered stoves to replace ones run on coal. Assuming the old ovens are taken out of service, then the new ones will reduce the amount of CO_2 being added to the atmosphere in the future. Offsets can also support schemes, such as regenerative farming, that actually draw down carbon back to earth. Both approaches are important and in need of financing, according to The Global Sustainable Tourism Dashboard's Susanne Becken, who says we need to 'stop putting more fossil carbon into the atmosphere and we need to bring the carbon back into the form of biomass as much as possible'.[11]

The other most common forms of offsetting involve trees, either planting new ones (afforestation) or protecting those already there by preventing deforestation. Preventing deforestation matters, because it stops further CO_2 from being released into the atmosphere. However, because the trees were already living and performing their role of absorbing carbon, it doesn't result in them increasing their activity. Planting more trees through afforestation does increase the total capacity for absorbing CO_2, but because trees grow slowly, it can take several years for the full benefits to be felt.

What impacts do offsets have on sustainable development?

Potentially good. If forests are protected through financing community ownership, then this can be a means to support sustainable livelihoods. Likewise countries such as the Seychelles are exploring Debt for Nature mechanisms, where the islands' national debt would be paid down by wealthy, more industrialized, nations in return for the Seychelles protecting its forests. When schemes support clean and efficient technologies, be they stoves or rooftop solar panels, adopting them can transform the lives of those receiving them, often women. These social co-benefits are a strong argument for investing in offsets – but only once you have reached a point at which you are unable to reduce emissions further that year.

Should hotels and other travel companies use them?

Yes, but again, only to supplement their efforts to reduce core emissions, never instead of doing so. 'One of the largest criticisms of the voluntary carbon offset market is that purchasing offsets will, at best, justify business as usual behavior and, at worst, actually increase emissions of CO_2', writes Matthew J. Kotchen in the *Stanford Social Innovation Review*.

> Although there is little research about the effects of purchasing offsets on behavior, the existing evidence suggests that people do not indulge in carbon emissions as a result of purchasing offsets. After all, the type of person who is willing to buy a carbon offset in the first place is likely to be quite green.

---

[11] Personal Correspondence, 11 August 2017.

I don't see too many Hummers on the road with window decals touting that the owner purchased carbon offsets.[12]

Once a company has done everything it can to reduce its emissions, and has in place a transformational programme to continue reducing and reversing them as fast as possible, it will almost certainly still be creating emissions that are worsening global warming, and whose impacts will be most felt by those who gained least benefit from fossil fuels. In addition, there will be all the emissions created in the years before any efficiency efforts were implemented, whether from building or operating our businesses. As CO_2 emissions affect our atmosphere for 100 years or more, the emissions we caused in the past decades are just as in need of addressing today as those we might create in the future. To fully tackle our climate impact, we need to take responsibility for and mitigate what we did in our past too.

Introducing Forum for The Future's recent *Offset Positive* report, the former director of Friends of the Earth and Chair of the UK's Sustainable Development Commission, Jonathan Porritt, asks:

> I have only one question: when you've done everything you can to reduce your own carbon footprint through changing your lifestyle and being super efficient at home, work and play, what are you going to do about the rest? Ignore it – or deal with it by finding the best possible offset product on the market?

German offset provider Atmosfair. de is a good place to start.

How should businesses communicate their use?

Transparently. Using shorthand such as 'carbon neutral' without further qualification does not tell anything like the full story. The implication is that the offsets have nullified the impact of an activity. 'We could technically cut down all the rainforests in Australia and offset the loss of carbon captured in Australia by planting new forests in North America to capture the same amount of carbon',[13] argues Michael Polonsky, Chair in Marketing at Deakin University. We'd balance net emissions globally, but have destroyed a rainforest.

Companies should disclose their actual emissions (along with the story of what they have done to reach that level). Then they can explain that because there are still a proportion of emissions that they are currently unable to stop, they are donating a proportionate amount of money to a carbon offset scheme. (Rather than seeking the cheapest offsets, they should finance reductions worth considerably more than the amount of emissions caused). Framed right, such transparent storytelling should be more powerful than a

---

[12] https://ssir.org/articles/entry/offsetting_green_guilt (accessed 30 July 2017).
[13] https://theconversation.com/carbon-offsets-saving-emissions-but-not-saving-the-environment-11429 (accessed 30 July 2017).

misleading label when it comes to communicating the challenges with and potential role of offsetting. Offsets should not be promoted as a standalone solution, nor should companies tell travellers that such actions have freed people to continue business as usual. Any suggestion that a hotel or tour company that offsets travellers' flights has somehow made these flights green or carbon-free is disingenuous greenwash. Companies should not be talking about 'offsetting emissions' so much as 'offsetting the emissions we have been unable to stop'.

How should hotels implement carbon offset schemes?

Hotel chain Accor uses a more circular approach known as 'carbon insetting'. The principle is similar to offsetting, except that the reductions come from inside a company's own operations and supply chains.

Accor says it is responsible for 18 million MWh of energy per year, with 75% of this consumption coming directly from the hotels themselves.[14] Working with Pur Projet, the chain now supports local schemes within its supply chain, such as a women-run olive oil business in Morocco that it helped set up and plant olive groves. 'Women in the area can have trouble finding work,' says Accor sustainable development manager, Arnaud Herrmann, 'so we provide the budget to plant the olive trees, the women of the region take care of the trees and transform the olives into olive oil, and part of the olive oil produced is sold back to our hotels.'

They also used the principle to redesign their towel reuse scheme. If guests reuse their towels, Accor reinvests 50% of the associated energy savings into tree planting close to their hotels.

This approach challenges a hotel to question which aspects of its complex supply chain it should consider part of it emissions and responsibility. If it outsources its laundry services, is it still responsible for the emissions? Would, for example, ensuring that its laundry service supplier used electric vehicles to collect and deliver the linen be a form of carbon insetting?

How about how and where their food is produced? Or the vehicles used by the tour companies the hotel chooses to promote? If tourism promotes itself as responsible for sustaining those jobs, then it is responsible for their impacts too.

How about the decisions made during construction? As Interface's carpets demonstrate, every product contains within it so-called 'embodied carbon', which is the CO_2 emitted during the manufacture, transport and construction of any building materials, together with end-of-life emissions.

Is your marketing budget focused on attracting international guests for whom a flight is the likely means of arrival? If so, should the emissions

---

[14] http://www.accorhotels.group/en/commitment/sharing-our-knowledge/our-footprint (accessed 31 May 2016).

caused by guest journeys count as part of a hotel's total embodied impact? Soneva thinks so, and factors them in, charging guests a 2% climate levy on top of their room stay to pay for their emissions. Since being implemented in 2008, the levy has raised US$6.2 million, which has been invested in reforestation projects in Asia and the Myanmar Stoves Campaign, which has mitigated 388,599 tonnes CO_2 to date, while providing 186,018 people with fuel-efficient stoves in Myanmar and Darfur alone.

Such offsetting projects can transform lives. Soneva's project is the first CDM Gold Standard Foundation certified carbon project in Myanmar, a country with one of the fastest rates of deforestation in the world. Without access to these stoves, families cut down the forests for firewood. As the forests disappear, the price of wood gets higher, driving more and more families into energy poverty. Cutting expenditure on wood makes a huge difference to families already living in poverty, and reducing time spent gathering wood means freeing up more time to spend on smallholdings and securing a good harvest.

Can we design hotels that move beyond carbon neutrality as a goal?

'Net-positive organisations recognize that it is not enough to seek to be "less bad"', says Elisabeth Filkin, Associate Director in Upstream Sustainability Services at JLL, which specializes in real estate and investment management. 'In the absence of real and lasting government action, businesses increasingly have a moral imperative to adopt a restorative approach to put back more into society and the planet than they take out.'[15]

Many hotels are well positioned to produce a significant amount of energy on site using sustainable means. Finolhu Villas in The Maldives is said to be the world's first 100% solar-powered five-star resort. It has its own solar panels that generate more power than the resort generally needs, with any excess energy stored for rainy or cloudy weather. There's also a desalination tank ensuring it is self-sufficient in water.[16]

Whatever energy needs hotels cannot supply themselves should be sourced from the most sustainable energy supplier possible. Battlesteads Hotel uses UK green energy supplier Ecotricity. Not only does Ecotricity source all the energy it supplies from renewable sources such as solar and wind, it also continually invests in building more clean energy sources, meaning that the money a customer spends with it doesn't just buy already accounted for green energy, it also helps increase the amount being produced

---

[15] https://www.hospitalitynet.org/news/4082948.html (accessed 31 May 2017).
[16] http://inhabitat.com/this-jaw-dropping-luxury-resort-is-100-solar-powered/ (accessed 31 May 2017).

Fig. 2.3. Belgian hotel chain Martin's 'Eco-Bon' scheme rewards guests for supporting their circular economy initiatives.

(and by extension, counters demand for fossil fuels). In Italy and Spain, all of Melia's hotels are on tariffs from energy companies delivering energy from renewable sources.[17]

Several of the world's largest companies, from industries as varied as IKEA, Apple, Nike and Facebook, have signed up to RE100, committing to use 100% renewable energy by 2020. The only company working in tourism to be part of the initiative is Vail Resorts, the world's largest mountain resort operator, which joined in 2017. None of the world's largest hotel or tour companies were on the list on 1 September 2017.

Acknowledging that sourcing renewable energy can be a complex challenge for hotels with buildings in many locations, the Norwegian company ECOHZ has developed a framework to make it possible. 'Just as we now expect hotels to encourage guests to reuse towels and save water,' reads their website, 'ECOHZ is certain that it won't be long before customers, investors

[17] http://www.greenhotelier.org/our-themes/energy/melia-hotels-100-renewable-energy-in-italy/ (accessed 31 May 2017).

and other stakeholders simply expect hotel groups to document their renewable energy consumption.'

It has also developed an initiative that not only enables hotels and other companies to buy renewable energy, but also to support additional production. If a hotel group signs up for its GO2 scheme, then every time the group purchases a MWh of renewable energy, part of their fees will be invested in funding renewable energy projects that are ready to construct but require financing.[18]

There are other ways to help reduce emissions. For hotels with the budget to invest, they could make a statement with something like a CityTree – a high-tech green moss wall that scrubs the air of harmful particulates and purifies as much air as 275 urban trees, removing 240 metric tons of CO_2 a year. So far 20 CityTrees have been successfully installed in major cities around the world at around US$25,000 each. For those with less money available, painting your roof white is a cheap, quick and effective first step, with a study finding that increasing a roof's reflectivity from 10–20% to around 60% can cut a building's cooling costs by more than 20%, significantly reducing emissions if adopted worldwide.[19]

What role do guests have to play in reducing carbon emissions?

While hotels should not shift responsibility onto guests, they can look for ways to engage them in their efforts. Park Hotel in Ljubljana, Slovenia has a series of large images of the country's national parks hung on each of its eight floors. Each image is accompanied by a QR code, and when a guest has walked up all the flights of stairs rather than taken the lift, and scanned all of the codes, they are entitled to a free drink in the ground floor cafe, and are also informed of how many calories they have burned off and how much energy they have saved. At House of MG in Ahmedabad, India, each room's energy consumption is measured, and if guests stay within a certain limit, they are rewarded with vouchers to be spent in the hotel's restaurant, or its gift shop, which is stocked with handicrafts made by local artisans. At Martin's, their version of the loyalty scheme is called Eco-Bon. If guests request a limited cleaning service for their room, they get 20 Eco-Bons. Reusing their bath towels gets them a further 10. Some dishes in the hotels' restaurant are labelled EcoetBon as they contain locally sourced, seasonal ingredients, and the short delivery distances from suppliers reduce CO_2 emissions. When guests have accumulated enough Eco-Bon points, they can be cashed in for free meals, accommodation and other experiences at various Martin's properties.

---

[18] https://www.ecohz.com/renewable-energy-solutions/go2/ (accessed 28 June 2017).
[19] https://link.springer.com/article/10.1007%2Fs10584-008-9515-9 (accessed 28 June 2017).

Can we support our communities towards clean energy?

A truly carbon-positive hotel would not be one that simply bought up a surfeit of carbon credits, but rather designed its building and processes in such a way that through a combination of on-site energy production and efficiency measures, the building was able to feed renewable energy that it had produced back into the grid. It's perfectly feasible to design such buildings. In 2015, the first carbon-positive house in the UK was built at Bridgend in Wales, hardly an area known for its endless sunshine.[20] In Lyon, the Hikari development is a 12,800 square-metre mixed-use development of offices, shops and housing that produces more energy than it consumes thanks to its own vegetable-oil fuelled co-generation plant and solar panels.[21] The Muottas Muragl hotel in the Swiss Alps is a rare example of a hotel that produces more energy on site than it needs.[22]

As well as sharing the extra energy they create, hotels that are working towards – and achieving – truly transformative energy shifts should share what they learn not just with guests, but with people who live nearby. Hotels can act as progressive hubs by sharing knowledge, inviting students in, providing advice to local businesses and community groups, or sharing toolkits and best practice advice.

The Three Glens is a four-bedroom property based on a farm in Dumfriesshire, Scotland. Electricity is sourced from its own 100-kW turbine on the hill. Heating from its own ground-source heating. Food cooked on a biomass stove. Water from its own borehole, heated by solar thermal. There's a turf roof, insulation from the farm sheep's wool. 'The owners are happy to share all invaluable information they can to guests embarking on a similar eco-project', says the website. 'They'll disclose build costs, running costs, hiccups and challenges if you choose to stay here. And Three Glens will demonstrate that sustainability without carbon-burning is about more than just installing the latest bit of renewable technology.'[23]

Can we achieve zero water?

For years, towel cards urging people to conserve resources have been the most common, and often only, way that hotels attempt to engage guests

---

[20] http://www.thecccw.org.uk/uks-first-smart-carbon-positive-energy-house/ (accessed 31 May 2017).

[21] http://www.onlylyon.com/en/news/inauguration-d-hikari-a-lyon-le-premier-ilot-mixte-a-energie-positive-de-france.html (accessed 28 June 2017).

[22] http://www.clean-energy.ch/fileadmin/user_upload_cleanenergy/user_upload/pdf/Muottas_Muragl_e_Flyer_Plusenergie.pdf (accessed 28 June 2017).

[23] http://www.3glens.com/about/green-appeal/ (accessed 28 July 2017).

with regard to sustainability. Despite their virtual omnipresence, they remain poorly utilized.

There have been numerous studies into what makes for the most effective approach. The most often cited research was conducted in 2008 by Goldstein, Cialdini and Griskevicus, who wanted to see whether social proof could increase customers' compliance with a towel reuse programme. (Social proof is the basis of us choosing to follow the crowd. We're more like to buy because 7 out of 10 cat owners chose it, or 85% of people who watched this film also liked…)

The researchers compared two approaches. The first was the industry standard approach, employing a message that dwelled on the importance of environmental protection. The second described a norm, informing guests that most other guests (75%) participate in the programme. Of those staying in rooms where the cards featured the descriptive norm condition, 44.1% reused their towels, compared with 35.1% of those in the rooms that focused on the environmental issues.

In 2017, TUI Benelux sustainability manager Melvin Mak placed towel cards with a variety of messages throughout a 700-room four-star hotel on Fuerteventura. Some of the guests were reminded about the environmental impact of their towel use, while other texts tested whether reinforcing habit would have more impact with the message: 'Reuse me again tomorrow. Just like at home.' The reuse rate for bath towels increased from 38.6% to 49.4% when guests were reminded how they acted at home.[24]

A range of other approaches have been employed. As described earlier, Accor plants trees. Radisson Blu funds clean water in Africa. For every 250 towels that guests reuse, the hotel chain will donate enough money to the charity Just a Drop to provide clean water for a child for life. Guests learn how many children were provided with drinking water through the hotel's in-bathroom cards, with Radisson Blu hoping to ensure 12,000 children have access to fresh drinking water each year. Ubic, which has two hotels in London and Amsterdam, simply offers its guests a free drink at the bar for keeping the towels an extra day.

Whatever approach is chosen, hoteliers need to ensure that any externalities are considered and the benefits are clearly communicated – to all concerned. In 2014, 200 protesters amassed outside Toronto's Sheraton Centre objecting that Starwood's 'Make a Green Choice' scheme was taking away jobs.

If towel cards epitomize limited ambition and exaggerated claims when hotels ask people to 'save the planet' through a small individual action, then the antithesis can be seen in the transformative approach to water management, and the communication of it, of the award-winning Chepu Ecolodge in Ecuador. Located in Chile, the lodge is entirely off grid. All of the water it

---

[24] https://www.tuigroup.com/en-en/media/press-releases/2017/2017-08-08-study-on-the-re-use-of-hotel-towels (accessed 28 July 2017).

Fig. 2.4. Chepu's resource monitors are sited across the hotel.

uses it collects through rainwater harvesting and filtration, gathering water in a 16,000-litre well and two 5000-litre tanks. In 2013, the lodge won the water conservation category at the World Responsible Tourism Awards.

Despite the finite amount of water available, their website also asks guests not to bring plastic bottles, and requests that anyone who does brings them takes them away again. A water management system tracks exactly how much water (and energy) is being used, and in-room tablets inform guests of their usage set against a recommended level that the lodge's re-sources can sustain. There is also a screen in the main hall that displays the information for anyone to see.

When guests check out, they are rewarded for remaining within their Eco Limits. They are given a choice – Chepu plants a tree on their behalf in Patagonia, or offers them a financial equivalent as a discount. Less than 1% of guests exceed the suggested maximum amount of water.

Chepu's approach seems radical, until you consider what had happened in Cape Town in 2017. By late May, the city's reservoirs sank to an effective 10.5% of their capacity after five years of drought. According to the *LA Times*:

hotels have taken steps to reduce water usage, asking guests to use hand sanitizers instead of water, limit use of towels, not to run taps when cleaning teeth or soaping hands and to limit the length of showers. Some hotels provide place updates on the dam levels in guest rooms to encourage water economy. Hotels are installing water recycling systems and water restrictors on taps to cut water flow.[25]

Can hotels provide clean water to communities?

Hotels operating in countries that will suffer increasingly from drought and pressure on limited water resources over the coming years need to consider how they will be perceived by the local community if they are seen to be taking more than their fair share. The most transformative hotels look beyond reducing their own water demands, exploring ways they can improve access to clean water for surrounding areas. Kasbah De Toubkal, a remote lodge in Morocco's Atlas mountains, levies a 5% surcharge on all guest stays that has been used to fund a range of community initiatives, including improving access to clean, safe water in nearby villages. Jicaro Island, a Nicaraguan ecolodge, has installed a filtration system that provides safe drinking water for the local school and community of 600 people. Ol Pejeta is an award-winning group of safari lodges, camps and a conservancy in Kenya's Laikipia dryland areas, which works with local farmers on conservation agriculture, rainwater harvesting and carbon sinks projects. It provides training and resources to support greenhouse-based farming and drip irrigation techniques that mitigate the need to extract water from rivers, while increasing crop productivity.[26]

How to move from a 'waste less food' to 'waste is food' mindset

The US Environmental Protection Agency (EPA) diagram (see Fig. 2.5 on the next page) shows how industry should approach its attitude to food and waste. For this upside-down pyramid, traditional waste approaches, namely landfill (where it contributes to the production of methane, a greenhouse gas 21 times more potent than CO_2) and incineration, are at the bottom, with composting just above.

As we saw with rethinking a hotel's approach to waste in general, the EPA considers that the most important approaches – Source Reduction and

---

[25] http://www.latimes.com/world/africa/la-fg-southafrica-capetown-drought-20170523-story.html (accessed 1 June 2017).

[26] http://www.olpejetaconservancy.org/community/infrastructure-projects/water/ (accessed 27 June 2017).

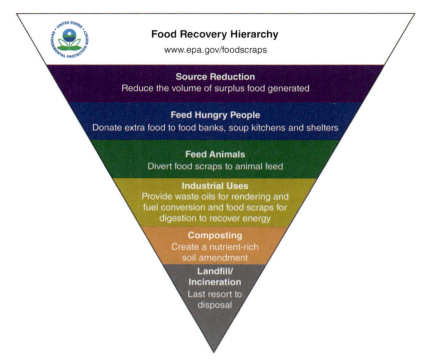

Fig. 2.5. The EPA's Food Hierarchy chart ranks the effectiveness of various approaches to addressing food waste.

Feed Hungry People – require designing the waste out of a system in which currently two-thirds of food wasted in the hotel and restaurant sector is perfectly edible.

In 2012 NordicChoice hotels collaborated with consultants GreeNudge and climate scientists from CICERO on a study to reduce food waste. Fifty-two hotels were divided into three groups; one got smaller plates, one got information signs on the buffet table about food waste, and one served as a control group.

The hotels that featured information signs saw food waste drop 20.5%. But even without informing guests of the issues, the hotels that provided them with smaller plates reduced food waste by 19.5%. With around 22,000 guests visiting its hotels every day, NordicChoice calculated that if all their hotels were to adopt smaller plates, it would reduce food waste by 613 tons each year, reduce annual carbon emissions by 1166 tons and save the hotel chain 31 billion Norwegian kroner. Significantly, NordicChoice reported that 'Guest satisfaction remained unchanged for all groups'.[27]

---

[27] https://www.nordicchoicehotels.com/social-responsibility-in-nordic-choice-hotels/the-food-revolution/matavfall/ (accessed 27 June 2017).

Having reduced the amount of food being ordered and consumed, the next most significant approach, according to the EPA, is to 'Feed Hungry People'. This might be donating surplus food through organizations that work with local charities, such as the UK-based PlanZheroes, a social network that facilitates relationships between food businesses and charities to ensure food reaches those in need, safely and conveniently. Elsewhere the Helsinki-based ResQ Club has created an online platform enabling locals and tourists to buy restaurants' surplus meals for a discounted price (typically 40–60%). Since launching in early 2016, ResQ has signed up over 150 restaurants and hotels in the city. 'We are a food rescue service', says ResQ CEO Tuure Parkkinen. 'We enable restaurants and hotels to advertise their leftover food portions that are still in great condition, but which need to be consumed that day.' Another rapidly growing initiative is being promoted by a few enterprising individuals and by the Solidarity Fridge Network, with examples I know of in Spain, India, Germany and the UK. In principle it simply means putting a working fridge in a publicly accessible place, where anyone can leave or take food for free. In the UK several leading food suppliers are supporting the schemes as a way to avoid throwing away waste, and there is no reason why hotels couldn't do the same.[28]

The third level of the EPA's hierarchy is 'Feed Animals'. A University of Cambridge study found that turning food waste into pig feed could free up 4.4 million acres of farmland and reduce costs by up to 50%. According to the EPA, in Las Vegas, a city rarely associated with sustainability, the MGM Grand now recovers 14,000 tonnes of waste food that previously went to landfill and feeds 3000 pigs each day.[29] In the Danish hotel group Guldsmeden, all food waste is sent for recycling for production of biodiesel and biogas, the next tier down on the EPA's pyramid.

Composting comes low on the EPA pyramid, but integrated with growing healthy, organic vegetables, salads, herbs and fruit it provides an essential part of closing the food loop. Guldsmeden also sends its used coffee grounds to Beyond Coffee,[30] a project that uses them to grow organic mushrooms, which the hotel buys. Strattons, a 14-bedroom boutique hotel in England, dries the used coffee granules naturally and offers them to guests and the local allotment society for use in their gardening. The scheme removes 332 kg from its waste stream each year, and helps guests and local people grow more food.[31] In just one year (2010–11), Strattons saved over £16,000 through reducing its food and related packaging waste. Alongside

---

[28] http://www.huffingtonpost.co.uk/trewin-restorick/community-fridges_b_17540904.html (accessed 27 June 2017).
[29] https://www.epa.gov/sustainable-management-food/links-and-resources-about-food-recovery-las-vegas (accessed 28 June 2017).
[30] http://www.beyondcoffee.dk/ (accessed 2 June 2017).
[31] http://www.wrap.org.uk/sites/files/wrap/WRAP%20-%20Strattons%20case%20study%20-%20FINAL.pdf (accessed 27 June 2017).

Fig. 2.6. Hotel Verde grows salads on the wall outside the restaurant.

increasing recycling levels to 98%, the hotel reduced food waste, explains WRAP, 'by cooking to order, using fresh produce including fruit and vegetables grown in the gardens, sourcing meat from a local butcher and eggs from free-range chickens on site'. Thanks to its efforts, now less than 2% of the hotel's waste is sent to landfill.

Can hotels grow their own food?

Of course any hotel with a garden can grow food for its guests. But so can those that don't. In 2014, the prize for the Hotel of Tomorrow award at the European Hotel Design Awards was won by a concept called The Edible Hotel. As hotel sustainability website GreenHotelier explained:

> the design features an open-plan lobby space which merges the reception, kitchen and bar areas of the hotel with an 'edible wall' and aquarium at its heart. The structure of the 'wall' uses the vertical farming technologies of hydroponics and aquaponics to theoretically produce enough food to subsidise two thirds of the hotel's meals.[32]

This may have been a winning concept in 2014, but it is perfectly feasible today. Located near Cape Town airport, Hotel Verde's vertical hydroponic system supports 475 plants, providing organic vegetables to be used in the kitchens for guests.

City-based hotels can connect to and support similar initiatives offsite too. Grow Up is a London-based start-up producing food for the hospitality sector and other clients, using aquaponics and vertical farming in an indoor controlled growing environment. The nutrient-rich waste-water from the fish tanks is pumped to the roots of the plants where microbacteria convert the waste into helpful nutrients, which then fertilize the plants , which in turn purify the water.[33] Likewise Growing Underground, also based in London, sustainably grows fresh micro greens and salad leaves 33 metres below the streets, with a hydroponics system that uses 70% less water than traditional open-field farming, and all nutrients are kept within the closed-loop system.

In both cases, because the food is so locally produced, it can be in the hotel kitchen very soon after being picked and packed, providing the freshest vegetables possible. Such schemes are viable in cities across the world.

How can hotels help guests enjoy climate-friendly food?

According to *Drawdown*, 'the most conservative estimates suggest that raising livestock accounts for nearly 15% of global greenhouse gases emitted

---

[32] http://www.greenhotelier.org/our-themes/new-builds-retro-fits/edible-hotel-design-addresses-food-sustainability-issues-of-the-future/ (accessed 2 June 2017).
[33] http://growup.org.uk/aquaponicsverticalfarming/ (accessed 2 June 2017).

each year; the most comprehensive assessments of direct and indirect emissions say more than 50%.' And it is set to get a lot worse. A 2016 report from the World Resources Institute says the world is on course to demand nearly 80% more animal-based foods, and 95% more beef by 2050.

Adopting vegan and vegetarian diets, on the other hand, says a 2016 study by the University of Oxford, could reduce business-as-usual emissions by as much as 70%, while also reducing global mortality rates by between 6 and 10%, saving over US$1 trillion in annual healthcare costs and lost productivity, and upwards of US$30 trillion when accounting for the value of lives lost.

NordicChoice Hotels has a section on its website stating that the chain commits to 'serve less red meat to contribute to healthier guests, a better environment and less climate change', with supporting statements linking red meat consumption to obesity, cancer and climate change.[34] In Guatemala, Laguna Lodge Eco-Resort & Nature Reserve was voted one of the world's 25 best lodges by National Geographic Travel in 2013. Yet despite the fact that 95% of Laguna's guests are omnivores, the lodge doesn't serve any meat or fish.

Nonetheless, many hotels fear guests will be resistant to words like vegetarian or vegan. The World Resources Institute has recently launched the Better Buying Lab initiative to explore ways to increase people's purchasing of plant-based foods. It is supported by several leading companies, including Hilton. It is still in its early stages and is focusing on three key themes.

1. How do we break with traditional habits of describing plant-based foods and do so in a positive way that appeals to meat- and non-meat eaters alike?
2. How do we popularize dishes based on vegetables, legumes and other plants and ensure they appear on more menus?
3. How can companies and other organizations track environmental benefits of diet shifts over time, and know if shifts are ambitious enough to meet global environmental goals?[35]

According to the Better Buying Lab, the focus of communication should not be on providing more information about relative climate impacts of different food choices. Rather, it should communicate the diversity of tastes and textures and colours of vegetables to diners. When most menus go no further than tacking on an uninspiring mushroom risotto or penne arrabiata, the vegetarian alternative is presented as a dull afterthought, a quota met and little else. Instead menus should include the meat-free dishes in

---

[34] https://www.nordicchoicehotels.com/social-responsibility-in-nordic-choice-hotels/the-food-revolution/mindre-kjott/ (accessed 28 June 2017).
[35] http://www.wri.org/our-work/project/better-buying-lab/three-areas-innovation (accessed 7 June 2017).

with the other mains on the menu, rather than separating them off into a vegetarian section, as this has been shown to boost take up, as does promoting one or more vegetarian dish as a chef's recommendation. Until it closed in late 2017, London's Grain Store restaurant did all of these, describing its dishes so that the vegetables are presented as the key ingredient, even those that include meat.

In Denmark, Guldsmeden explicitly connects ethical food with high quality for its guests. All its hotels have achieved the highest standards issued by the Danish government, and their website states:

> The harder it is to achieve, the easier it is to maintain. This has been our experience. Being subjected to scrutiny that leaves no stone unturned, means that we are now at liberty to focus on our good atmosphere and hostmanship, and not worry about whether we have been thorough enough in our sustainability efforts.[36]

The juxtaposition of 'scrutiny' and 'liberty' also addresses framing issues around tourism and responsibility. Where most say they make ethical purchases 'wherever possible', Guldsmeden's purchasing policy (clearly accessible on their website) makes their absolute commitments transparent:

> We aim to buy only organic food/drink, and will choose another product if unavailable in organic form. On rare occasions, if a minor item is unavailable in organic form, we will purchase a locally produced and sustainable equivalent. This is never meat or dairy. We do our best to keep appraised of current recommendations regarding the use of seafood, and to adhere to these in our restaurants. We never serve seafood on the WWF red list.[37]

Hotels can also help protect vulnerable species (such as those on the WWF red list) by promoting the consumption of invasive creatures threatening their survival. For example, in the Caribbean the invasive lionfish is putting at risk the survival of the coral reefs, and reducing native fish numbers by up to 80%. The Travel Foundation is working with local hotels, restaurants and fishermen in St Lucia to develop supply chain networks and create communication materials that encourage the catching and eating of lionfish.[38]

The Slow Food Movement is also committed to preserving endangered species, but its approach turns this on its head, focusing instead on promoting their consumption. Originally launched as a campaign to stop McDonald's from setting up a fast food establishment by the Spanish Steps in Rome, it has grown into a global movement to protect and promote some of the rarest, most unique foodstuffs on the planet. These are animal

---

[36] https://guldsmedenhotels.com/wp-content/uploads/2016/09/GuldsmedenHotels SustainableManagementPlan.pdf (accessed 2 June 2017).
[37] https://guldsmedenhotels.com/wp-content/uploads/2016/09/Guldsmeden-Hotels-purchasing-policy-final.pdf (accessed 2 June 2017).
[38] http://www.thetravelfoundation.org.uk/project/lionfish-on-the-menu/ (accessed 2 June 2017).

breeds and edible plant species that exist in small numbers, often in very small areas. As they are not deemed commercially viable, their numbers dwindle. Yet because they are reared and farmed by small-scale, sustainable, organic means, preserving and promoting them does more than ensure their survival. They are at the heart of networks of sustainability – both environmental and cultural – promoting biodiversity in local farms and districts, sustaining farmers and others working in traditional and more sustainable ways, helping preserve knowledge of traditional dishes and festivals that grow up around such foods, and attracting visitors.

Does your menu support your local community?

As Slow Food has always understood, food offers an introduction to different cultures. Slow Food UK has an initiative called Forgotten Foods, which encourages people to reconnect and discover 'Britain's unique food heritage'. Hotels can support marginalized local communities by engaging them as chefs and thus enabling guests to discover cuisines they might otherwise not have access to. At London's Mazi Mas restaurant the chefs are migrant women, who previously would only have the opportunity to cook in their homes. Meanwhile restaurants such as Fifteen in the UK and Koto in Vietnam have been set up specifically to provide culinary and hospitality skills to disadvantaged young people.

Situated just outside Bangkok, the Sampran Riverside hotel extends the model to working with local farmers. Through its on-site organic farm it has developed and sent trainers out into the surrounding country, helping 80 local farms convert to or produce food organically. The hotel alone sources approximately 8 tonnes of organic vegetables, fruits and herbs and 3 tonnes of organic rice per month from local farmers for its restaurants and spa. It also oversees a network of other buyers, together ensuring a sustainable market for the farmers' produce. It also collaborates with local schools, setting up organic vegetable plots in their grounds to promote organic farming for the children's health and understanding of sustainability. It has opened a weekend farmer's market on the hotel grounds for the farmers to come and sell their produce. Guests can also tour the hotel's own farm, or visit farms it has helped set up.

Grootbos is a luxury hotel and reserve found in South Africa's Cape Floristic Region, where it has restored and now manages 2500 hectares of very high conservation value land, with 785 indigenous plant species recorded on the reserve, of which 117 are species of conservation concern and seven are endemic to Grootbos. Its Growing the Future project provides skills development in organic agriculture, sustainable animal husbandry and beekeeping, with a particular focus on educating women. The farm is run as a commercial enterprise to provide an income for the Grootbos Foundation projects – all vegetables, herbs, lettuces, fruit, eggs, honey and preserves produced at this

Fig. 2.7. Grootbos's Greenfutures supports sustainable farming and provides local employment.

farm are sold back to the Grootbos lodges. It also runs food security projects, in particular the innovative 'Green Box' home garden system, which provides local families with the resources to grow their own food.

At Three Tree Hill Lodge, also in South Africa, guests pay 20 rand per night to the social community fund, part of which is spent providing children at the village pre-school with vitamin-enriched porridge on a daily basis. The donations have also enabled the hotel to build a jungle gym at the school, significantly boosting attendance, to set up a computer room with internet access at the high school and to develop a permaculture garden and environmental learning centre for children and the villagers.

Can your hotel act as a network hub?

Although unmeasurable in terms of actual impact, if every hotel guest who asks for advice is told the simplest ways to use public transport, connected to taxi companies using hybrids, provided with walking maps (designed by the hotel to highlight sustainable and community-focused businesses and experiences), and recommended restaurants providing local, ethical food and shops supporting authentic arts and crafts, then a hotel can genuinely offer a transformative experience.

At Canada's Fogo Island Inn, every guest is 'matched' with a local who will help show them round the island. According to the Inn:

> Our community hosts are passionate, lifelong Fogo Islanders who are pleased to offer their insights into the Island's natural and cultural heritage. They have fished the Island's shores, picked its berries, climbed its rocks, driven its roads, and walked its trails hundreds of times over. They are intimately connected to their home and eager to pass on their extensive knowledge of Fogo Island's culture and history to our guests.

The Arlo Soho in New York offers guests complimentary bike rides by subsidising bike hire from a local shop. Hilton London Bankside has partnered with a local business, Bamboo Bicycle Club, which trained the hotel's staff how to build six guest bicycles out of sustainable bamboo. At London's QBIC hotel, space is given over to Cafe Art, an organization that aims to reconnect people affected by homelessness with society through art. They now run their charity from the hotel's basement and are given wallspace to showcase some of their artists' work.

At the Indian boutique hotel chain CGH Earth, the staff of Coconut Island hotel clean the neighbouring village of rubbish every other week. And Hotel Verde in Cape Town positions a clothing bank in the lobby where guests can donate clothes they don't want to take home which the hotel distributes to local community groups.

Tourists already hire ski boots when they go skiing, so Sweden's Rent-a-Plagg has extended the idea, now enabling visitors to hire all the necessary kit. As most people need ski equipment for a week or less each year, such hire schemes maximize the material's use. Hotels could also look to support local circular economy initiatives, such as Amsterdam's 'Fashion Library' LENA, where members pay a monthly subscription to enable them to borrow vintage and designer clothes. In principle, guests could travel with less luggage (making the journey easier and reducing emissions) and enjoy wearing different clothes while on holiday. 'Our dream is to go on holidays with some hand luggage and your library card, and have access to a big LENA wardrobe wherever you are', says co-founder Suzanne Smulders.[39]

Hotels could also connect with circular initiatives to attract local residents into their premises. In London a project called Library of Things enables members to borrow a wide range of items as diverse as kitchen equipment and musical instruments that are only needed once in a while, as well as offering one-on-one instruction and workshops to learn how to use things such as power tools and sewing machines. In Frankfurt, the Tool Library rents out tools, which most only buy and then use for a few minutes a year.

Hotels could provide a home for such initiatives, their workshops or other education initiatives. Since 2014, 2500 children have been taken

---

[39] https://www.fastcompany.com/3045366/at-this-fashion-library-you-check-out-clothes-instead-of-buying-them (accessed 2 June 2017).

round Cape Town's Hotel Verde during off season to see its various initiatives and learn of the challenges they are designed to address. Basecamp, a safari lodge in the Maasai Mara, also operates as a learning centre, hosting more than 300 college students each year who are taught how an eco-camp operates. Chumbe Island, an ecolodge located off Zanzibar, has provided environmental education to thousands and created teaching resources now used in the national curriculum.

In the Gambia, Geri Mitchell and Maurice Phillips have founded the Sandele Eco-Retreat and Learning Centre. As well as being a hotel, the retreat is a 'living demonstration centre' for alternative technology systems and techniques while also supporting the environmental and economic development of the surrounding villages. It is also one of several hosts across the world for the Global Ecovillage Network's Ecovillage Design Education course, which teaches about the ecological, economic, social and cultural challenges that the world – and its villages – is facing, as well as providing training in practical responses such as water conservation, how to construct more efficient wood-burning stoves, and setting up local co-operative ventures. The villages it works with (eight in The Gambia and three across the border in Senegal) have gathered together as The People's Coast Ecovillage Network, collaborating towards transforming into ecovillages and joining the Global Ecovillage Network.[40]

Why hotels should stop treating staff like externalities

The key to many of the initiatives mentioned so far, whether advising guests on great local experiences, encouraging a more plant-based diet, running successful energy conservation measures, or radically rethinking a hotel's attitude to waste, lies with the staff. Yet too often they are treated like an externality, where instead hotels should be adopting a more circular approach to their recruitment and retention.

People leaving the industry need replacing each year (at considerable cost in terms of hiring and training). In the UK, around 993,000 new staff will be needed by 2022, of which 870,000 will simply be replacing existing employees. Low pay is the main reason given, with the hospitality and tourism workforce contributing just £21,600 per employee to productivity each year, compared with £46,000 per head in retail and £52,000 in manufacturing.[41]

In 2015, The Unethical London report into working conditions in the UK capital's hotels found that despite room prices in the city rising by an

[40] https://www.travindy.com/2016/08/interviews-with-tourism-social-entrepreneurs-10-maurice-phillips-from-sandele-foundation/ (accessed 2 June 2017).
[41] http://www.people1st.co.uk/insight-opinion/people-and-productivity/the-skills-productivity-problem-2015/ (accessed 2 June 2017).

average of 7.3%, and hotel profitability increasing by 2% each year, 68% of hospitality workers were being paid less than the London Living Wage.

Women suffer the most from these conditions. A report into employment and the tourism industry in Brazil[42] showed that the average earnings in the country's tourism sector for men were 43% higher than for women. As the International Labour Organization wrote in 2010:

> A divergence between qualifications and workplace reality is observable for women, who make up between 60 and 70 per cent of the labour force. Unskilled or semi-skilled women tend to work in the most vulnerable jobs, where they are more likely to experience poor working conditions, inequality of opportunity and treatment, violence, exploitation, stress and sexual harassment.

Nor are gender imbalances limited to those workers at the lower end of the pay scale. Women own less than 10% of the hotels around the world. They make up less than 10% of corporate boards in hospitality companies. And according to the *Global Report on Women in Tourism 2010* by UNWTO, only one in five of the world's tourism ministers is a woman.

Many big hotel chains have excellent diversity strategies in place, with the likes of Marriott recognized as one of the 100 Best Workplaces for Women.[43] But even these initiatives only go so far. As the 'Women in Tourism & Hospitality: Unlocking the Potential in the Talent Pool' white paper puts it, there may be:

> Aspirational and laudable corporate policies in major hospitality companies that support opportunity for women on an equal footing to men and, in some cases, provide additional affirmative action to enable women to progress in organisations. However, such policies and programmes rarely extend to include the increasingly diverse and extended supply chain that is in place in companies that outsource services across a range of front- and back-of-house functions.[44]

Wolwedans is a luxury tented safari camp in the Namibrand desert in Namibia. There are few opportunities for employment in the remote villages scattered across the region. Where many hotels see outsourcing of such services as a way to separate themselves from responsibility for how their operations are managed, Wolwedans is using it as a way to extend the impact of its sustainable business model. It is developing the Maltahöhe Village Laundry Project to manage its laundry using fewer natural resources and less energy, while creating jobs. The project will employ local women and Wolwedans will set up a natural wastewater treatment plant to provide safe,

---

[42] http://www.ipea.gov.br/portal/index.php?option=com_content&view=article& id=2967 (accessed September 2017).

[43] http://fortune.com/best-workplaces-for-women/ (accessed 2 June 2017).

[44] https://www.diageo.com/en/investors/financial-results-and-presentations/women-in-tourism-and-hospitality-white-paper/ (accessed 2 June 2017).

non-potable water to irrigate a self-sustaining garden and orchid project and grow vegetables, as well as provide gardening skills.

Initiatives like this that support girls and women in education and into meaningful work also have a little-acknowledged yet highly significant effect on efforts to reverse climate change. A 2010 economic study found that investment in educating girls is 'highly cost competitive with almost all of the existing options for carbon emissions abatement – perhaps just $10 per ton of carbon dioxide'.[45] Another 2013 study found that educating girls 'is the single most important social and economic factor associated with a reduction in vulnerability to natural disasters'.[46] Project Drawdown assessed educating girls to be the sixth most powerful tool for reversing climate change.

If underpaying staff results in under-trained, under-engaged employees who need replacing and retraining, then the opposite approach offers a virtuous circle, where sustainability can play a key role. A study of hotels in Hong Kong reported that hotels keen to develop sustainability programmes should assess potential staff's attitudes as early as the interview stage, and then ensure adequate training is given to employees. While this may seem onerous, it added that one advantage of hiring employees who 'personally follow ecological environmentally friendly practices' is that there is a greater chance of them being more committed to their jobs, since they will be eager to work for environmentally responsible companies.[47]

The Good Group runs a floating hotel currently moored in London's Docklands and a boutique guesthouse in Guatemala. At both properties, their Good Training programme offers custom-made hospitality training to unemployed people. Successful trainees get on-the-job training and a full-time salary at the hotel, after which they are supported in finding a permanent job in the local economy. The company also reinvests all its profits in developing its model and increasing its impact.[48]

As well as only employing local staff, Cambodian hotel Soria Moria runs an employee ownership scheme in which the employees have become partners and majority owners of the business, now accounting for 51% of shares, with the hotel making clear that its 'long term goal is to explore ways to transfer the remaining 49% of the business to the local employees'. The hotel also runs yearly staff training trips throughout Cambodia for staff to learn more about their own country and what it has to offer. As the hotel explains, this is a 'combined reward, team building and hands on learning

---

[45] https://www.cgdev.org/files/1424557_file_Wheeler_Hammer_Economics_Pop_Policy.pdf (accessed 2 June 2017).

[46] https://www.ecologyandsociety.org/vol19/iss1/art42/ (accessed 2 June 2017).

[47] https://www.researchgate.net/publication/261292157_What_drives_employees%27_intentions_to_implement_green_practices_in_hotels_The_role_of_knowledge_awareness_concern_and_ecological_behaviour (accessed 2 June 2017).

[48] https://www.good.community/impact/ (accessed 2 June 2017).

experience about how it is to be a tourist (most Khmers can usually not afford to travel and experience this on their own expense)'.[49]

Also in Cambodia, Sala Bai is a six-room hotel, spa and restaurant. Guests are asked to be patient with the staff because most of them are trainees. In 2002, French NGO Agir pour le Cambodge set up the Sala Baï programme as a way to address poverty and human trafficking in the country by providing hospitality training for young underprivileged Cambodians. Each year its hotel and restaurant school provides a free education in hospitality for more than 100 students, with a priority given to girls, who make up 70% of the intake.

All training fees, supplies and uniforms and all daily expenses, such as accommodation, food and medical, are covered by the school, for all students. In the final month of their year-long course the school helps them find a job, with a 100% success rate to date. And thanks to their training, their starting salaries are on average three times higher than their family's average income, meaning that once they have qualified, they are in turn able to support siblings and other family members through education and into work.

Koto (which stands for know one, teach one) is a social enterprise that runs a growing number of restaurants and hospitality training schools for disadvantaged young people in Vietnam. Its founder Jimmy Phan opened his first sandwich bar in 1999, and within two years had another restaurant and had set up his training school. Hundreds of thousands of customers later, the Koto enterprise keeps growing, with international guests coming not only to eat but to learn, either through cooking classes or on social enterprise study tours, where they can learn about the challenges and rewards of setting up such schemes.

In Austria, Vienna's Magdas Hotel is located in a restored old people's home, and filled with upcycled furniture such as wardrobes from the compartments of old Austrian Federal Railway trains. It is also a social enterprise where two-thirds of its staff are from refugee backgrounds. 'For people with a refugee background, it is still difficult to find work in Austria', says its homepage.

> Initial lack of German language skills, the resentment of many employers, as well as the circumstance that refugees are only allowed to accept work after receiving a positive response to an asylum application (which can often take months or years) make integration difficult.

In Spain it is mandatory to reserve 2% of jobs for people with disabilities. Illunion hotels won the People category at the WTTC Tourism for Tomorrow awards in 2015 for going way beyond this statutory requirement. Of the 500 people who work in its hotels, 10% have some kind of disability. They work everywhere from reception to floor supervision, human resources to administration. The company has recently set up two of its hotels as 'Special Employment Centres'. At these two properties, 70% of the staff are disabled in some way.

---

[49] http://thesoriamoria.com/responsible-tourism/good-business-practice-in-soria-moria/ (accessed 12 May 2017).

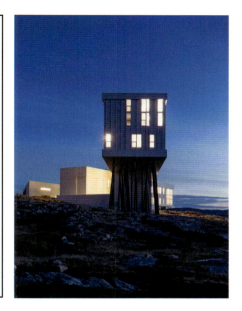

Shorefast Label for Economic Nutrition ©
fogo island inn

Actual 2016	Where the Money Goes
Ingredients	% Financial Value
Compensation	50%
Food & Room Supplies	14%
Commissions & Fees	5%
Operations & Admin	16%
Sales & Marketing Expenses	5%
Surplus Reinvested in the community of Fogo Island	10%

Economic Benefit Distribution

Fogo Island	63%	Canada	22%
Newfoundland	8%	Rest of World	7%

Fig. 2.8. Fogo Island Inn's Economic Nutrition labelling brings transparency to its relationship with its supply chain and local community.

In the Italian city of Asti, all the staff at the 21-room hotel Albergo Etico have an intellectual disability of some kind. On the top floor of the hotel is its Independence Academy, where the participants of the project live during their three-year internship period. During this time, they learn the skills of the tourism trade, along with skills for living independently. As they become experienced, trainees mentor new arrivals who, as they progress through the programme, feedback into the programme's development by doing the same.[50]

* * *

Hotels should be as transparent as possible about the benefits of the way they choose to operate. In 2016 Hub Kathmandu organized an event with the women owners of the Panauti Community Homestay. They wanted to teach them something about media, about the value of guest relations, and how the community homestay programme was developing. This simply meant sharing with them the reviews on TripAdvisor, reading them aloud to women with no other access to these results.

The Statler Hotel at Cornell displays pictures with stories about hotel staff, many of whom are students training in hospitality at the university. Kasbah du Toukbal in Morocco lines the walls of its hotel with photographs of its staff and stories of their lives. Canada's Fogo Island Inn was set up as a 100% social business. All operating surpluses are reinvested in the community of Fogo

---

[50] http://www.albergoetico.asti.it/accademia-e.php (accessed 12 May 2017).

Island through the projects and programmes of Shorefast Foundation. Perhaps its most original and transparent initiative is its use of what it calls 'economic nutrition labelling'. As the hotel explains:

> Most people are accustomed to seeing nutritional labelling on the foods and beverages they purchase. These labels allow consumers to make conscious and informed decisions about their food choices. Food nutrition labelling was revolutionary for the food industry. Now, we want to spark the same energy for change with the launch of economic nutrition labelling.

A bill at Fogo describes what percentage of a guest's contribution goes to the staff, how much to its charitable foundation to invest in social projects and how much of it remains in the local community.

Make sure your hotel is open to everyone

Over the course of this chapter, I have drawn together examples from across the world to imagine what a truly transformative hotel might look like. The underlying principle I have repeatedly returned to is that of shifting from a wasteful and inefficient linear approach to an inclusive, circular one. For maximum impact, therefore, a hotel needs to also be open to the widest range of guests possible. This starts when it is constructed, or restored, and one of the guiding principles is universal design.

Universal design addresses issues around accessibility. But it moves beyond a hotel just making sure it has a certain number of 'accessible rooms'. Rather it looks to produce buildings, products and environments that are designed to be universally enjoyed by anyone, regardless of their accessibility requirements. For those needing persuading of the business case, worldwide the accessible tourism market is 1.3 billion people, which because they often travel with friends and family, represents a market of 2.2 billion people.

One of the forerunners in hotels has been Scandic, with its Design for All methodology. Whenever a new hotel is opened, staff spend time moving around it in a wheelchair so as to get a better understanding of the experience. It helps them see where small adjustments are necessary, such as cleaners ensuring the shower nozzle is in reach. More significantly, Scandic has made Design for All's 135-point checklist and online training openly accessible to anyone, regardless of whether they work at the company or not.

To be truly transformative, tourism must help shift societies from a concept of meeting accessibility obligations to one of inclusivity and universality. It is a shift in mindset from ensuring your restaurant has one special table adapted for wheelchairs, to making design and purchasing decisions that mean all tables are built to allow wheelchair access. As the late disability activist Scott Rains asked: 'What if the first question we asked was, "What is so unique about this situation that it justifies exclusion?" instead of, "How much does it cost to make it accessible?"'

Transforming Travel Experiences   **3**

Imagining what it is like to be someone other than yourself is at the core of our humanity. It is the essence of compassion, and it is the beginning of morality.

Ian McEwan

'To say I hate township tours is an understatement', writes South African blogger Sabelo Mkhabela. 'I loathe to witness tourists being dropped off in busloads 'to see how people live'. It's treating the township like a zoo and it's plain disrespectful. It invades people's private spaces, with strangers taking pictures of them while they try to go about their daily routines.'[1]

Mkhabela lives in a predominantly white suburb of Cape Town. In 2015, he got together with a couple of photographer friends to create a video to 'flip the township tour on its head' by taking pictures of people in the suburbs going about their daily lives – drinking in bars, walking their dogs, playing with their children.

This creates an unsettling film. The people from the poor neighbourhood come into the richer district and take photographs. The objects of the black photographer's camera become angry and assert their rights not to be filmed and framed as passive objects of someone else's gaze.

An alternative approach that addresses these imbalances can be found in the work of Reality Tours, which has been working in Mumbai's largest slum since 2006. Residents of Dharavi guide visitors on walking tours designed to show how the slum is the heart of small-scale industry in Mumbai. Guests get to see recycling, pottery making, embroidery, bakery, a soap factory, leather tanning, poppadum-making and much more. However, to avoid the sort of problems exposed by Mkhabela's film, groups are kept small, have to comply with a strict and respectful dress code, and most importantly of all, photography is not allowed. The company now also runs tours

---

[1] http://livemag.co.za/featured/watch-viral-video-camps-bay-suburb-reverse-township-tour/ (accessed 12 June 2017).

in Delhi's Sanjay Colony, and advises tour operators around the world, such as Smokey Tours in Manila, the Philippines.

Eighty per cent of Reality Tours & Travel's profits go to community development projects run by its sister NGO, Reality Gives. These include circular economy initiatives such as a women's empowerment scheme turning old saris into designer products, as well as a girls' football programme, and a computer course it designed and whose curriculum it made open source and shared with other NGOs across Mumbai and Hyderabad. In the Philippines, meanwhile, Smokey Tours invests 100% of the proceeds from its slum tour in a local NGO that assists local communities with disaster relief and preparedness.

South African blogger Busisiwe Deyi suggests the issues that need resolving go beyond ensuring tourists behave respectfully when visiting disadvantaged communities:

> If the tours are to have a 'social justice' component which has any chance of surviving beyond the allocated three hours, the tours need to move into the neighbourhoods of the observers and expose the segregation, poverty and marginalization which exists in those spaces.

I took a walking tour a couple of years ago in Sydney with the indigenous-owned tour company, Dreamtime Southern X. My guide didn't take me to look at dot paintings or hear a didgeridoo recital, but rather to stand on the site of the Rocks in Sydney Harbour and look at the bridge, opera house and other iconic buildings that a tourist is unlikely to connect with Aboriginal Australia, and to try to see the significance of these edifices that I had long taken for granted through her eyes and through the history of a people dispossessed to make way for them.

Pointing to the Sydney Opera House, she told me how it had been constructed on land that had for centuries been the site of an Aboriginal shell midden – a place where they discarded empty shells once they had eaten their contents. They used this pile of shells as a visual reference point to what they had been eating, and therefore how plentiful their food stocks were. It helped them manage their resources sustainably (one of countless examples from across the world of indigenous people's knowledge and belief systems embodying circular, nature-based understanding). Apparently the largest of these 'shell monuments' were up to 12 metres high and covered half an acre.[2]

When the British arrived, we didn't look to understand the meaning of the shells, so crushed them up for use in the construction of the buildings around the Rocks area, and in the foundations for Sydney Harbour Bridge. My guide told me that when she looked at the Opera House's iconic shape, it didn't make her think as most tourists do of sails, but of shells. In fact, the architect Joern

---

[2] http://nationalunitygovernment.org/content/every-important-colonial-building-sydney-was-placed-upon-significant-first-nations-city-site (accessed 4 July 2017).

Utzon was influenced by the history of the shells when creating the building's design; when a memorial to him was unveiled in 2009, an Aboriginal welcoming committee presented his children with an ochre-painted shell.

Since 2013, Migrantour has been creating a European network promoting intercultural walks around some of Europe's most visited cities. The walks are guided by migrants from old and new generations, so as to show tourists, students and locals their neighbourhoods as they perceive and experience them. One guide, Sara – who was born in Turin of Egyptian parents – takes women to see the city's Peace Mosque from her perspective, while introducing her guests to Islam as she lives it today. Another, Bangladesh-born Madhboi, guides groups through the alleyways of the Torpignattara neighbourhood in Rome, taking them to sari shops and food emporia, before visiting a Bangladeshi Association to meet with the women there and learn about how they continue their customs and traditions in the Eternal City.

Dan Glass set up Queer Tours of London in 2017 to make visible the history and ongoing struggles of the LGBTQ+ community in a city that tends to pride itself on being inclusive. The walks look back at the likes of the Piccadilly Circus 'Dilly Boys' and their renegade hand-wiggling flirting-code, the Adelphi Theatre's 'Notorious Urinal' and make less expected stops such as Harley Street to reflect on how homosexuality was once classified in the UK as an illness. 'We wanted to bring a deeper sense of history and therefore belonging, affirmation, identity and ultimately empowerment to our community. Every street of London has a story to tell. The good the bad and the ugly', explains Glass.

> The tours serve three main purposes. To shine a light on London's rich LGBTQ+ history through creative, audacious and life-affirming interactive walking tours, give a better understanding of our queer history to build for our queer future, and generate people power and financial support for London's queer campaigns.[3]

For cities in particular, the surfaces of gay and immigrant cultures are increasingly appropriated into the presentation of the tourism spectacle. Such tours serve to remind participants that the chance to enjoy the world's cuisines in the likes of Soho is set against the ongoing struggles for acceptance of both immigrant and LGBTQ+ communities. No one, however, attempts to appropriate the life of homeless people into some sort of transgressive chic. But who better to understand a city than someone who lives on its streets? For the past several years Unseen Tours have employed homeless men and women as guides to the streets of London. Their model has been emulated in cities across Europe.

---

[3] http://www.independent.co.uk/life-style/london-first-lgbtq-history-tour-dan-glass-soho-vauxhall-gay-lesbian-transgender-bisexual-a7493011.html#gallery (accessed 4 July 2017).

Fig. 3.1. Unseen Tours provides unique insights into life on London's streets.

They took me around some of the most visited places in London – Borough Market, The Globe Theatre and Tate Modern – yet the insights I was given were completely new. My guide told me of the Banksy mural painted over when the chain restaurant took over. Pointed out how certain benches and stretches of pavements I had passed hundreds of times were designed to deter rough sleepers. Made me see differently a space I thought I knew well.

Too often tour companies assume tourists only want to see happy faces and a charade is enacted to gloss over more uncomfortable truths. Colonial houses and plantations are presented uncritically as 'Great Houses' where wealthy aristocrats once lived, the focus being on the beauty of their surroundings and possessions, rather than on them as the headquarters of the slavery that enabled their lifestyles. Which story of Jamaica will a tour company seek to tell – one framed through the experience of the colonists, or one that gives agency to those who were there before, who resisted and who remain now?

A 2017 article in *Forbes Travel Guide* titled 'Why Singapore's colonial past is a big tourism pull today' is typical of this way of framing our past. It describes the island's colonial history as:

Traders and immigrants came to this free port from across the region, and from as far as China and Europe. Foundation was laid for shophouses, bungalows and landmarks like Fort Fullerton (1829, where Four-Star The Fullerton Hotel Singapore sits now), Victoria Theatre and Concert Hall (1862) and Raffles Singapore (1887) – iconic addresses that still stand today.[4]

Theohilus Kwek challenges this perspective, writing in the *Singapore Journal*:

> Just as Singapore would not be the country we know today without its traders and merchants, it would be a very different place without the forced labourers who built our first roads, worked on plantations, or served the families of those traders and merchants for a pittance, or for nothing at all. By removing them from our history – or celebrating them selectively, as with the smiling portrayals of samsui women at the National Day Parade last year – we've set a powerful precedent for excluding today's forced labourers from our national community. It's easy to think about those who are blatantly underpaid and abused in our society as 'foreign', when we've always thought about them that way.[5]

Companies like South Africa's Fugitives Drift re-examine our history through multiple perspectives. For years the Rattray family, which owns the lodge in South Africa's KwaZulu Natal, has sat with elders in the local Zulu community and scoured imperial archives to piece together the many interpretations and events that led up to two epochal 19th-century battles between the British and Zulus that took place nearby – Isandlwana and Rorke's Drift. Over the course of a visit there, various guides take guests to visit the site and tell the stories of these battles. Some are white South Africans of English or Afrikaans descent, others Zulus. Each brings a slightly different perspective.

In 2012, Mejdi Tours was the first recipient of the UNWTO's Intercultural Innovation Award. It operates tours at places across the world marked by deep-seated conflict and often seemingly irreconcilable worldviews. It designs its tours using a two-guide model that equips groups with two local guides, each representing unique cultural, religious, political and ethnic narratives. Originally launched in Israel and Palestine as a dual narrative tour where Mejdi travellers are guided by one Palestinian and one Israeli, it offers trips using this approach in the likes of Cuba, Kurdistan and Ireland. These tours facilitate unique and privileged encounters. For example, in Bosnia and Croatia the trips involve experiences such as dinner with a former Bosnian general who now runs an educational NGO or conversation in Sarajevo with Christian and Muslim families once divided by the war.

---

[4] http://blog.forbestravelguide.com/why-singapores-colonial-past-is-a-big-tourism-pull-today (accessed 27 July 2017).
[5] https://singaporepolicyjournal.com/2016/04/11/a-history-worth-remembering-forced-labour-and-national-identity-in-singapore/ (accessed 27 July 2017).

Fig. 3.2. Mejdi Tours' Palestinian and Israeli guides use tourism to develop a shared narrative.

How can we transform how tourist and guide interact?

Dave Martin founded Bulungula, a remote backpackers lodge on South Africa's Wild Coast, to enable the local community to find ways of earning money that didn't rely on the men going off for months at a time to work in the mines. Despite their lack of experience with tourism, Dave ensured that the lodge was developed in ways that the people of Nqileni village were happy with, so that they would one day own and manage it. Several years after setting it up, he handed full ownership of the lodge back to the community.

From the beginning, however, rather than present himself as an outside expert telling the locals what to do, he encouraged them to come to him with their ideas, which he would enable, using the lodge as a bridge between them, their ideas and the backpackers. For example, one of the village's women offers guests an experience that provides an insight into her daily life. She is not a passive object to be looked at or photographed. She has created the tours she wants to give through collaboration with her guests, meeting them on her terms and exploring with them ideas for how she might develop her tour further.

This peer-to-peer tourist development can also be seen in the village of Ban Talae Nok on the coast of Thailand, which was devastated by the tsunami of 2004. Through the community company they have set up, Andaman Discoveries, they are developing collaborative tourism products. Guests who come to the village stay with families in their homes, helping replant mangrove forests, collaborating in batik workshops, learning to cook traditional dishes, playing with the children and sharing fish barbecues on the beach.

When I was there, guests spent time in the craft centre, not simply buying 'local handicrafts', but instead collaborating with the women, learning from them how to make soap, polishing coconut shells to serve as soap dishes, and providing suggestions on what tourists might expect. This isn't 'volun-tourism' where tourists come with a mission to help those they perceive as in need of external aid. Instead it is designed to promote seeing one another as equals – at Ban Talae Nok guests and villagers co-create products and experiences.

In Cape Town, AWOL offers a more participatory alternative to the standard Township Tour, with the bicycle tours it runs in collaboration with the Bicycle Empowerment Network in the township of Masiphumelele. Guests come as individuals or in very small groups, and their visit is con-ducted on bike or, where necessary, on foot. Not only does running the tours on bikes remove the physical barriers and disparity in scale a coach places between tourist and the people we visit, it also establishes a sense of mutual trust and equality.

The bikes themselves are shared by both tourist and resident, as AWOL uses the tours to fund the purchase of second-hand bikes for the commu-nity and to train local people as bike mechanics. The bicycles make it easier for the men and women of Masiphumelele to get the many miles from the township to work – or look for work – in the parts of Cape Town that inter-national tourists see more often.

Although many of the tours mentioned in this chapter are designed to ensure the presence of tourists benefits our hosts, they do not do this by sending people abroad to be volunteers. In recent years the criticisms of volunteering while on holiday – often known as voluntourism – have in-creased. Arguments against the practice vary, but include the fact that short-term volunteers can never fully understand a situation and so can only offer limited assistance. Using international volunteers to do tasks that could be achieved by local people takes jobs away from those that need them. And it does nothing to address any structural issues causing the problems in the first place.

Where children are involved – whether in orphanages or not – there are specific concerns over the potential for abuse; for children's develop-ment being affected by an ever-changing roster of people appearing in their life, loving them then leaving again; and as above, causing problems where rather than supporting family structures, a dynamic is created whereby chil-dren can be seen as a means towards financial gain.

PEPY Tours started out as a standard voluntourism company, offering the chance for visitors to come to Cambodia to support education pro-grammes by sharing their skills. However, its founders felt that they – and the volunteers they brought over – were making little impact on the devel-opment issues they were trying to address. Rather, they started to see that the most important 'contribution' of the volunteer was not what they did in

Cambodia while they were volunteering, but what they went on to achieve as the result of their learning and how it impacted on their careers and their lifestyle choices.

So they turned their volunteering model on its head, spearheading a growing movement known as 'Learning Service'. Coined by PEPY's founder, Daniela Papi-Thornton, the term reverses 'Service Learning' (which is a learning strategy that integrates community service so as to enrich the learning experience). The principles of Learning Service are as follows: rather than coming to communities – in this case in Cambodia – with the aim of helping, people on PEPY Tours experiences come to learn about the specifics of local issues, and also about the wider context such as international development, aid and global citizenship. 'Instead of turning up in a country having already decided that your role is to help, with a "problem" and "solution" that is fixed before you get on the flight,' says Claire Bennett, PEPY Tours operations manager, 'why not come to a country open to learning about the problems and solutions first?'[6]

How can we ensure tours have positive social impact?

Gopinath Parayil has always resisted voluntourism, arguing that if people want to volunteer, they should do so at home where they understand the conditions better, and let local communities build their own capacity instead. Rather, he wants tourists to come, to spend their money and to learn. In the southern Indian state of Kerala, his company The Blue Yonder has been pioneering transformative experiential travel since it was set up in 2006.

The company brings small groups of individuals to visit with local artists, entrepreneurs and cottage industries such as potters, sari makers and bell-metal craftsmen. Many of these men and women are among the last of their trade, and without the renewed interest shown by the Blue Yonder's tours, and the money they bring in, these trades and art forms may well have died out altogether. Because they live off the beaten tourist tracks they otherwise gain little or no benefit from Kerala's popularity as a destination.

The Blue Yonder brings guests to meet with people such as 68-year-old Ramankutty Kothavil, the last remaining practitioner of the art of making the 'koppu' – the intricate headgear and accessories, including bracelets, anklets, ornate vests and even weapons, that are integral to the staging of the traditional performing art forms of Kerala. Or the only practising bell-metal worker who makes the 'Adakkaputhoor Kannadi', a glazed metal mirror unique to the region.

---

[6] https://www.travindy.com/2017/04/reinventing-voluntourism-interview-claire-bennett-pepy-tours/ (accessed 2 July 2017).

When I first met Parayil in 2008, his company was one of the few connecting social enterprise and tourism. Now, such projects are proliferating and, thanks to dedicated online platforms showcasing them, it's getting easier to discover them. One such platform, Vayando.com, connects tourists with local entrepreneurs in emerging economies around the world. With a commitment that at least 50% of the entrepreneurs it represents will be women, Vayando looks to support them in their initiatives without creating a risky and unsustainable reliance on tourism. For some, gaining two or three bookings a month for a few hours at a time can double their income without disrupting their schedule so much that they are unable to focus on their core work.

In a similar vein, Visit.org's platform connects travellers with local social organizations around the world offering immersive experiences which align with the organizations' missions, and guaranteeing that 100% of the fee remains in the communities where it is spent. Like PEPY Tours, it reverses the traditional model of voluntourism; instead of the visitor providing a service to the local community, the local community provides a service to the visitor in the form of an immersive experience. So popular has its offer been, that a third of its guests book another activity within a week of their first experience.

Visit.org is one of a small number of tour companies (others include Mejdi Tours and the Spanish urban tour company, Authenticitys, along with hotel company Qbic) that have become a member of B Corp, 'a growing global movement of people using business as a force for good', and employing the B Corp system to measure and publish their social and environmental impacts. Unlike most other certification schemes used in tourism, B Corp is not focused solely on the travel industry but rather on all sectors; and where most schemes measure how much a business has reduced its emissions, waste and other negative impacts, it looks to measure the positive impacts it has as well. Authenticitys uses the B Corp certification scheme to benchmark its own progress, and since this results in its own impact report being publicly available, this gives the company the licence to ask suppliers and other partners to be able to measure and account for their own impact as well, thus nudging them towards transformation too. 'We believe in being part of a movement with one common goal: to change and redefine business to be a force for good', writes Authenticitys founder Elena Rodriguez Blanco. 'We believe in system transformation and we want to revolutionise business.'[7]

Groups like Authenticitys, Vayando and Visit.org are broadening ideas of what can be experienced in the name of tourism, seeking to create richer experiences for tourists while supporting those working for a more sustainable world. In Berlin, guides from Green Fashion Tours and GreenMe Berlin run a Circular Economy Tour, offering to 'knock on the doors of sustainable transition spaces, urban farmers, guerilla gardeners, circular designers and

---

[7] http://www.authenticitys.com/blog/certified-b-corporation/ (accessed 2 July 2017).

passionate food-savers, visit workshops and ateliers, a glimpse into alternative upcycling concepts, learn about the future of food and take a sneak peak into Berlin's handbuilt hub for social, cultural and environmental change'.[8] If Bill McKibben's assertion that the most useful thing that tourism can do is to show people other ways of living and acting is to be realized, then increasingly our ideas of what might make for tourism experiences will need to develop on these lines.

This may also mean that tourism – at least certain aspects of it – is finally embraced by many of the most progressive, innovative projects exploring ways of living more sustainably. Many of these offer tours, and are eager to share what they do with interested visitors, but would baulk at describing this as tourism. Yet for the tourist seeking a new way of discovering a place, these 'non-tourist' organizations can offer innovative and original experiences.

There's the New York-based Museum of Reclaimed Urban Space, which works to preserve the history of grassroots activism in the city, guiding people on tours of the many subcultures and alternative movements that have sprung up over the decades. Or Bread, Print & Roses, a UK-based creative collective that explores new thinking and fresh approaches to living. It wouldn't consider itself tourism – yet as well as publishing 'seditious pamphlets' and holding workshops in 'anarchist baking', they lead walks such as the 'From Industry to Arcadia' tour, which

> explores the back streets of Bath, exploring the city's divided history, and the mutual and co-operative solutions that have flourished in the margins, asking the question: 'What lessons might we take from the past that could accelerate ecological and social revival today?'

Perhaps the most developed of these explorations into ways of living sustainably – along with the Global Ecovillages Network – is the Transition Towns Network. Launched in the English town of Totnes in 2006 to explore how a community can work together to develop positive and low carbon ways of living, it has now spread to hundreds of villages, towns and boroughs across the world. It says its purpose can be summed up as 'increasing local resilience, reducing energy use and building a regenerative local economy through relocalization, and the promotion of regenerative development'. Yet despite there being a tours section on the Transition Towns Totnes website, for example, there is little on the network's central websites and in its literature investigating how tourism might play a part in such a future. In a 2009 paper looking at the possible connections between tourism and Transition Towns, Anna Waddilove wrote:

> There is uncertainty amongst groups as to how to integrate tourism into the Transition model, yet many of the existing working groups set up within

---

[8] https://www.goodevents.eu/iframe/de/events/circular-economy-tour-dinner-the-wedding-edition (accessed 19 September 2017).

Initiatives have relevance to tourism – if only the link is made. There is evidence to suggest that Transition Initiatives could offer an holistic approach to tourism development and that tourism could play a key role in linking many of the core elements of sustainability at the heart of Transition (and sustainable communities more widely) to drive change and promote sustainable development.[9]

Everyone accepts that there are forms of holiday experience where people learn to paint, to cook or to develop new skills. There's no reason why the industry's potential for sharing and spreading ideas for building a more sustainable world can't rapidly develop. To become truly transformative, it has to.

How can we offer transformative experiences to everyone?

When the UNWTO declared that the theme for World Tourism Day in 2015 was One Billion Tourists, One Billion Opportunities, they were looking at 1 billion as a big number. But in a world of 7 billion people, 1 billion international travellers means 85% of the world did not take an international holiday in 2015. If we truly believe that tourism can be transformative, then we are obliged to do what we can to spread its benefits way beyond a highly mobile elite, and make it accessible to as wide a number of people as possible.

Based in Northern Botswana, the company Endeavour Safaris takes guests – regardless of disability or access needs – on luxury, tent-based mobile safaris. They are also opening a fully inclusive lodge, designed so everyone can enjoy the thrill of the bush. And in India, Planetabled has looked to bring an open, collaborative approach to offering fully accessible holidays. All of its trips are designed to be accessible to all people, regardless of disability, bringing people with widely divergent experiences together.

What happens, however, where accessibility is not a physical issue, but a financial one? Travel companies need income to survive, meaning there is little incentive to open up their experiences to those who can't afford to pay. However, over the last couple of years, a few companies, such as the US travel company Elevate Destinations and UK-based responsibletravel.com, have been exploring one possible approach. Emulating the 'Buy one give one' model made famous by Tom's shoes, where each purchase funds an equivalent 'gift' for a disadvantaged person, it is the first time such a model has been used by the travel industry.

For each trip sold, a local travel experience will be donated to disadvantaged young people. In African countries, for example, where poaching

[9] http://www.transitiontownwestkirby.org.uk/files/Anna_Waddilove_Survey.pdf (accessed 31 July 2017).

Fig. 3.3. Elevate Destinations' 'Buy one give one' tour concept opens up the thrill of travel to those who would otherwise not get the chance. (Courtesy of Elevate Destinations/Unique Costa Rica, Altos del Roble School.)

is threatening the existence of many of the animals upon which inbound tourism to those countries is based, it is hoped that enabling local people, and children in particular, to experience the pleasure of watching these animals can assist in their protection. According to Elevate Destinations President Dominique Callimanopulos,

> It is a fact that few locals have the means to visit the very sites that makes their countries attractive to tourists, who spend a lot of money traveling to those sites every year. I felt that offering the same opportunity to local youth sends a message of equanimity, empowerment and equal opportunity to local communities and provides both an educational perspective and feeling of ownership of national resources for those communities.

Transforming Places

4

Let us imagine that the enormous sums of money spent every year on travelling for pleasure were used for the embellishment of our cities and landscapes, the improvement of our workplaces, the search for a harmonious life! Let us imagine that the charm and beauty of holidays could trickle into everyday life. Then all the problems of tiredness and the need for recuperation would be solved by what I propose to call the 'solution of the heart'. No more holidays or – if you like – endless holidays. True life, genuine happiness.

Michel Tournier

What do we mean by place?

A place demands two things – geographic space and a human relationship. As William Kittredge writes in *The Nature of Generosity*:

> Places come to exist in our imaginations because of stories, and so do we. When we reach for a 'sense of place,' we posit an intimate relationship to a set of stories connected to a particular location, such as Hong Kong or the Grand Canyon or the bed where we were born, thinking of histories and the evolution of personalities in a local context.

Like human relationships, these deepen over time. We may first be struck by the surface-level beauty, but as we spend longer, we discover more. I do not say this to devalue a tourist's experience. It is the wide-eyed wonder of novelty that thrills us as travellers. Likewise, our familiarity with the places we know well can cause complacency or inertia, making it harder to imagine things being different. Tourism can jolt us into the unknown. It offers the freedom from our daily concerns that can come from being somewhere different, somewhere where the most mundane experiences take on special significance. Travelling by underground at home is to bemoan the proximity of other commuters. As a visitor to Tokyo it becomes a spectacle. 'For some Europeans I know, an American superhighway is an attraction of the first rank,' writes Dean MacCannell in *The Tourist*, 'the more barren the better because it is thereby more American.'[1]

These experiences all have value, for their own transitory thrill but also for the way they illuminate our own routines, the ones that we will return to once our trip is over. Maybe we appreciate their own nuances a little more. Perhaps we see them differently, become more aware and less willing to accept their inadequacies, and so motivated to make change.

What is the difference between place and destination?

Tourism favours the word destination, often defined by little more than a checklist of key landmarks and activities. We are lured to London for Big Ben, red buses, the Changing of the Guard. To the Serengeti to tick off the Big Five.

Destination evokes the grandeur of destiny, and the expectant drama of travel towards a final, defining, goal. The more often one visits a place, on the other hand, the less it feels like a destination. And no one uses the word to describe the place they call home.

Why does this matter? Because when we prioritize the promotion of destination over the preservation of place we end up with Venice. Hollowed out, overcrowded, somewhere to see once, on a short sojourn from the boat, a selfie in St Marks, pick up a trinket, tick it off and on to the next fix.

So unique a place is Venice – so defined by its canals and gondoliers – that it may seem an extreme example. After all, it has always been a tourist hotspot. In the late 19th century the American novelist Henry James wrote: 'Though there are some disagreeable things in Venice there is nothing so disagreeable as the visitors.'

Venice is a sinking repository of old stories. But it is also an overflowing petri dish for what is to come. The Acqua Alta is a high tide that strikes Venice on average four times a year. Google it and you get pictures of tourists dancing with water round their ankles, and tips on how to enjoy it – another spectacle, one more thing to tick off the list, a seasonal novelty like the Namaqualand Daisies or the Northern Lights. Except it is becoming less rare. And more destructive.

According to the *New Scientist*, a team of researchers studying the impact of climate breakdown and erosion on the city made a conservative estimate that 'by the end of the century high water could swamp the city between 30 and 250 times a year'.[2] The lead scientist described this as 'unsustainable aggression'. Venice would become unliveable and be abandoned.

---

[1] Dean MacCannell (1976) *The Tourist: A New Theory of the Leisure Class*, p. 106.
[2] https://www.newscientist.com/article/dn17668-climate-change-could-swamp-venices-flood-defence/ (accessed 12 June 2017).

Fig. 4.1. Is the Acqua Alta just another sight to be ticked off?

Unliveable for those who call the place home, although it's not hard to imagine that the cruise ships would still bring visitors to 'experience' Atlantis, and that Gondoliers would continue to ferry people around the sunken remains of the city, now stripped of its homes, restaurants, shops and people. At what point would the guides start telling a different story? When might tourists come to Venice not just to learn about its past, but to prepare for their future?

Why destinations become victims of their own success

Venice is one of the first names when we talk of places that have become overcrowded through tourism. But the list grows with each month. There are the icons, such as Machu Picchu, Barcelona, Cinque Terre. The new-comers like Iceland. And then those remote outliers which no one expected, from the Orkneys to the village of Point Lay (population 270) in Alaska, where so many have come to see the walruses that it has launched a reverse campaign urging tourists to stay away.

Point Lay's approach remains a rare exception, contrasting starkly with the standard tourism industry narratives that employ a fear-of-missing-out, 100 places to see before you die, scarcity + inadequacy model of marketing, which ensures people will continue to go to these places regardless of the dispiritingly ersatz version of themselves they might have become.

The perils of highlighting a limited 'bucket list' range of places' supposedly unique selling points is seen in the increasing resistance to the status of being declared a UNESCO World Heritage site. Although in principle it is awarded to iconic places to support their preservation, it can have the effect of exerting extra pressure on them through stamping them as touristic 'Do Not Miss This'.

In 1995, the Lao temple city Luang Prabang was awarded UNESCO World Heritage status. Although it is home to no more than 50,000 people, it was visited by more than 530,000 foreign and domestic tourists in 2014. A plot of land that would have sold for US$8000 before the surge in tourism can now command US$120,000. According to an article on the website Skift, 'most of the locals don't live here anymore'.

Writing in Matador, Mark Hay describes a visit to the Ethiopian city of Harar that had, on the one hand, seen civic services improve since becoming a World Heritage site, but where its residents – in an echo of the Alternative Township Tour – now complained of

> being watched, judged, and limited in their own homes. Forced to flash-freeze their interiors and exteriors, they also feel constricted in what they can do to improve their lives, from repairing damage to a façade to installing some new appliance.[3]

Unless they were constructed like Disneyland or a modern ski resort explicitly to cater to tourists, the places that we visit exist regardless of the presence of tourists. The dynamic of physical and social interactions that define the systems of their societies may benefit from the input of touristic energy through investment and cultural curiosity. Or they may struggle and warp should tourism distort them. An accommodation sector transformed along the lines I have imagined will support supply chains and community enterprises. So too will an approach to travel experiences that favours a range of local voices and interpretations. When it comes to seeking a regenerative role for tourism as regards the destinations/places where it operates, I believe it should be grounded in a humble effort to understand the inherent dynamics – whether of a human-designed city or a wild ecosystem – and seek primarily to support these complex networks' capacity to flourish.

How to ensure places flourish 1: regulation

Barcelona's Mayor Ada Colau has said no more licences will be granted for new rental accommodation in the city. Cinque Terre has begun issuing

---

[3] https://matadornetwork.com/pulse/city-gets-named-unesco-world-heritage-site-people-lose/ (accessed 16 July 2017).

a number of passes to limit access to its coastal paths. Berlin has banned Airbnb to protect affordable housing for Berliners. According to the author of *Overbooked*, Elizabeth Becker:

> Only governments can handle runaway tourism. Few major industries fall so squarely into their hands – local, regional and national. Governments decide who is eligible for visas: how many cruise ships, airlines and trains can bring in visitors, how many hotels receive building permits, how many beaches are open to development, how many museums and concert halls are open, even how many farmers receive subsidies to raise food for the restaurants and cafes that tourists frequent.[4]

Everything has a capacity. The number of predators in an ecosystem is defined by the amount of prey. A street can only take so many vehicles before it reaches gridlock. Numbers can be managed but only if we start from an acknowledgement of capacity.

If I phone up the theatre and all the seats are sold, I don't protest. I don't say I am willing to sit on the floor or the stairs. We all agree that the play would be spoiled through too many people trying to cram in. The chairs are there to regulate seating in the theatre – they improve the experience of those who are there, with an optimum number and price found to sustain the theatre's productions, while enabling people to come. If a play is popular, they extend the season. Or take it somewhere else. You can't move Venice, but you can work out – in concert with those who live and work there – what the capacity is, and then focus your strategies on not exceeding that.

How to ensure places flourish 2: taxation

The Maldives charges a so-called 'Green Tax' at US$6 per night in 'tourist resorts, tourist hotels and tourist vessels' and US$3 per night in guesthouses.[5] The Balearic Islands has also launched an 'eco-tax' of '1 euro per person per day, to those renting holiday property from private owners or those that visit the islands as part of a cruise – 2 euros per person per day, to those staying in high-end hotels or apartment complexes – 4 euros per person per day'. It is set to double in 2018.[6]

Officials said the Maldivian tax is to be spent on 'managing the waste from local resorts and other islands'. The Balearics said they would invest in 'environmental protection, sustainable tourism, the preservation and restoration

---

[4] https://www.theguardian.com/commentisfree/2017/aug/05/only-governments-can-stem-tide-of-tourism-sweeping-the-globe (accessed 14 August 2017).

[5] https://www.mira.gov.mv/GreenTax.aspx (accessed 14 August 2017).

[6] https://www.citizensadvice.org.es/faq/eco-tax-tourists-balearic-islands-doubled-1-1-2018/ (accessed 14 August 2017).

of cultural heritage, improvement of infrastructure in tourist areas as well as in research, training and development in the tourism sector.'

Many in the industry protested. 'Travel trade sees red over new green tax in the Maldives', declared TTG Asia. *Travel Weekly* called the Balearics tax 'a recipe for disaster'. People worried the bogeyman called 'taxes' might put tourists off coming.

It's worth challenging such assumptions. Suppose a cruise ship drops anchor off Mallorca for a couple of nights. The price of your cruise might go up by four euros. Or if a tourist was considering a five-star hotel – at a cost of several hundred, or probably over a thousand euros, then the price goes up by 14 euros for the week. Will they truly cancel and look elsewhere?

Suppose they would. Are they the sort of tourist the Balearics or Maldives want? Just how much money are these tourists going to put into the local economy once they arrive, if they object to spending two euros a day to protect and improve the very environment they are coming to see?

In the case of the Maldives, the evidence in favour of charging a sup-plement to protect the environment is already there. As I mentioned earlier, hotel group Soneva charges guests an extra 2% to mitigate the impacts of their flights and other activities. They don't call it a tax, however, but a levy.

An increasing number of places are introducing or contemplating tourist taxes of some form. New Zealand is proposing one to protect its environment. Iceland is looking to tax those who rent out properties through Airbnb. In Cambridge, Dr Sally Everett, deputy dean of the Business School at Anglia Ruskin University, suggests a different way of looking at using some form of tourism tax to protect the university city from being overrun by tourists in the summer, while also encouraging local people to more fully enjoy their home city.

> I would propose in Cambridge some kind of residents' pass to get a 10 or 20 per cent reduction on local attractions, food outlets and the whole tourism experience. I wouldn't call it a tourist tax. If you say 'we want a tourist tax' they think it will put tourists off, but actually it's a local reduction that locals pay less. I think there would be an appetite for local discounts.[7]

However such taxes are named and implemented, it is essential that clear environmental and social benefits result from them and that their commu-nication strategy ensures residents and visitors feel the benefits and see the connection. Get such a process right and the inhabitants of a place might see the presence of visitors as adding positively to their wellbeing.

How to ensure places flourish 3: intervention

What are the components of a great urban place, from a tourist perspective? Good accommodation, which meets the budget. Good places to eat, again,

---

[7] http://www.cambridge-news.co.uk/news/cambridge-news/tourist-tax-cambridge-prices-tourism-13463024 (accessed 17 August 2017).

at a price that suits. A transport network that works and is a pleasure to use. A feeling of safety. Air that is fit to breathe. An assurance that one is welcomed by the residents. Interesting – affordable – attractions, be they museums, galleries, churches, etc. Streetlife that is a pleasure to be lost in.

None of the above are unique to tourism – they are what make a place a pleasure to live and work in too. And the bedrock upon which they are built are decisions and investment by the local, regional or national government in terms of infrastructure and what means of navigating the city are prioritized. 'Our quality of life across the City Region must come first if we are to attract a renewed global market', writes Visit Manchester's 2008 report on its tourism development. 'We must be better for ourselves and only then will we know we have a product to be proud of.' [8]

One of the 100 solutions to climate change that makes it into *Drawdown*'s list is Walkable Cities, which

> enable people from all walks of life to get around, regardless of income, thus boosting equity and inclusion. With more people walking, traffic congestion – and associated stress and pollution – declines. There are fewer motor vehicle accidents. The more people walk (and cycle), the safer those modalities become. Increased levels of physical activity boost health and wellbeing, addressing widespread problems of obesity, heart disease, and diabetes. Social inclusion and neighbourhood safety rise, as do creativity, civic engagement, and connection to nature and place. Walkable cities are easier and more appealing to live in, making for happier, healthier citizens. Health, prosperity, and sustainability go hand in hand.[9]

Likewise, making cities cycle-friendly reaps many benefits. According to *Drawdown*, 'Copenhagen is considered the most livable city in the world, in no small part because it is the most bike friendly.' In the Danish capital, 30% ride to work, school and market on 18 miles of bike lanes, and along three bicycle superhighways connecting Copenhagen to the outlying suburbs. Traffic lights along the main roads are synchronized to the pace of bike commuters so they can maintain their cruising speed for long stretches. This is infrastructure designed to make locals' lives better, but that has huge benefits in terms of the tourist experience too, especially in the growing number of cities where there are bike hire programmes.

In October 2015, a progressive political alliance took control of Oslo's city council and announced that one its first priorities would be to make the Norwegian capital a more liveable and sustainable place. It set up a renewable district heating system and committed to drastically reducing the number of cars on the streets, which at the time accounted for 39% of the city's emissions.

---

[8] http://www.sciencedirect.com/science/article/pii/S0261517716300164#bib56 (accessed 20 June 20 2017).
[9] Paul Hawken (2017) *Drawdown*, p. 87.

The city announced plans to ban cars from the city centre, becoming the first major European city to have a total permanent no-car-zone. However, in response to resistance from certain shopkeepers concerned their business would suffer, the council has softened its plans – for now – and instead intends to in essence ban parking in the city centre by removing all of its on-street parking spots. 'We'll put up installations and create public spaces', Lan Marie Nguyen Berg, a Green party politician and the city's vice mayor for environment and transport, told the *Guardian*. 'Some will be playgrounds or cultural events, or [contain] benches or bike parking – or other things you can fill the space with when you don't have 1,200 kilograms of glass and steel.'[10]

In Tallinn, the capital of Estonia, they have subsidized free public transport for the city's residents by charging tourists to use it.[11] Car use has dropped, bringing down carbon emissions and making the streets more liveable for both residents and visitors. In Seoul, they have banned Uber but used similar tech to create an app supporting local taxi firms. The South Korean capital has also made unoccupied buildings and otherwise unused spaces available for meetings and citizen-led initiatives; made the city's policies and expense reports publicly accessible; boosted car sharing and children's clothing 'libraries'; and set up 2000 wireless access points in markets, parks and government offices. In Turin, capital of the Piedmont region that is the home of the Slow Food Movement, Mayor Chiara Appendino published a 62-page report in 2017 outlining how she intended the city to promote vegetarian diets so as 'to protect the environment, health and animals'.[12]

In 2012 the Slovenian capital Ljubljana was said to have the 'highest growth rate of overnight stays by tourists'[13] among European capital cities. In 2015 it won WTTC's Tourism for Tomorrow destination award for its promotion of sustainable tourism, and a year later was European Green Capital. It's also the only city to win the European Mobility Week Award twice and one of the ten cities in the Ellen MacArthur Foundation's Circular Cities Network.

In 2007, an ecological zone was created in the city centre, which as of 2012 was closed for motorized vehicles. In the past five years, pedestrian areas have been increased by almost 620%. Like London and Paris, it has a bike-sharing network – and here it is free for the first hour or for four hours to tourists buying a Visit Ljubljana card. An electric trolley-bus service called

---

[10] https://www.theguardian.com/cities/2017/jun/13/oslo-ban-cars-backlash-parking (accessed 8 June 2017).
[11] http://citiscope.org/story/2014/free-public-transit-tallinn-hit-riders-yields-unexpected-results (accessed 15 August 2017).
[12] https://www.theguardian.com/world/2016/jul/21/turin-mayor-italys-first-vegetarian-city-five-star (accessed 15 August 2017).
[13] http://www.eturbonews.com/28138/ljubljana-ranks-europe-s-top-3-tourism-growth (accessed 15 August 2017).

Fig. 4.2. Ljubljana's Kavalirs offer free, environmental friendly, transport around its city centre to everyone.

Kavilir provides free rides for anyone – but in particular the elderly, disabled or mothers with children – transporting hundreds of thousands of people around the historic centre in recent years.

By 2020 the city intends that public transport, non-motorized traffic and private vehicles should each account for a third of all transport. Whether you are a tourist or a local, such schemes make the city a more pleasant place to get around. 'Fears that this would kill local businesses never came to pass', wrote Simone D'Antonio in Citicscope. 'If anything, business and tourism have increased in the historic centre.'[14]

Ljubljana's efforts don't stop at sustainable transportation. It is the first EU capital to devise a zero waste strategy and already recycles two-thirds of its waste. There are grassroots civic initiatives to regenerate parks and create urban gardening projects, along with a Library of Things where citizens can rent out items they only need once. There's even a dispensing machine in the market square that sells fresh milk and cheese from the region's farmers.

---

[14] http://citiscope.org/story/2016/how-ljubljana-turned-itself-europes-green-capital (accessed 15 August 2017).

Tourism brings investment, but the city has been developed to support the people who live there first and foremost, and the municipal administration runs surveys and other initiatives to see how satisfied the people of Ljubljana are with tourism's impact on their city. As we shall see in Chapter 6, communication completes the circular approach, feeding people's thoughts, responses and experiences back into further development. 'Visitors feel comfortable only if citizens feel the same', says Petra Stušek, Managing Director at Ljubljana Tourism. 'We can achieve this only by working together.'

How to ensure places flourish 4: collaboration

Creating liveable cities does not of itself address issues such as overtourism. Imposing limits or taxes has a role to play, but they will always be fighting against the tide. In 2017, Copenhagen launched a new tourism marketing campaign that plays with a more inclusive, shared way forward.

'Wonderful Copenhagen concludes the end of the era of tourism, as we know it', announced the campaign.

> We pay our respects to the tourists of the past, the mass consumers and the passing days of disconnected tourist segmentation between business and leisure, city and countryside, culture and cycling. We bid farewell to an era of tourism as an isolated industry bubble of culture and leisure experts. We leave behind days of equating tourism marketing with glossy picture-perfect advertising. We recognize the expiration of our role as the destination's promotional superstar, the official Destination Marketing Organization (DMO) with authoritative consumer influence, broadcasting superiority and an exclusive right to promote and shape a destination.

In its place, the DMO proposed 'Localhood for everyone'.

Ljubljana asks its citizens what they want. Copenhagen invites visitors to see themselves as citizens for a brief while too. In both strategies, places are moving away from a consumer-focused model where the place is packaged

Fig. 4.3. Welcome Copenhagen's new tourism campaign reflects ongoing concerns about so-called 'overtourism'.

and sold as a destination to tourists to something much more collaborative, more circular, more modelled on natural processes.

Anna Pollock, the consultant and strategist behind the Conscious Travel movement and author of the groundbreaking report, *Social Entrepreneurship in Tourism – the Conscious Travel Approach*,[15] has for many years been exploring how this open-source, collaborative and networked approach to tourism destination development might work. In an interview with the destination marketing consultancy DestinationThink, she said:

> What we need right now are some conscious leaders willing to see tourism in their destination as a living, local, dynamic human system in constant conversation with its environment and comprising a host of self-organizing agents.
>
> The more we allow information and responsibility (the power to get things done) to circulate freely within that system the smarter it will become and the more it will flourish.[16]

How can nature teach better collaboration?

At 4229 square kilometres, the forests and rivers of Nam Et-Phou Louey are Laos's largest national protected area. Nam Nern, a safari operator working within the park, has come up with an innovative way to encourage the villagers who live within its boundaries to stop killing the wildlife, either for food or to sell on to illegal traffickers.

First, it employs villagers as guides. At the end of each safari, guests record what animals they saw. The villages are then remunerated (into a communal development fund) depending on what tourists see, with rarer animals worth more. All the members of the 14 villages that partner the lodge are signed up, and should a villager break the law and poach, the funds are reduced.

It's an elegant example of how to factor negative externalities back in to make a system more resilient. Poaching offers an individual the chance of gain, but with each animal that is extracted, the system is weakened (in terms of biodiversity, as a tourism experience since the chance of seeing animals has reduced, and also as a funding mechanism for the villagers, since fewer animals seen means less money). On the other hand, when the community works together to stop poaching, the integrity of the system is reinforced, as increased biodiversity makes for more sightings, resulting in more money for the community fund.

In Rwanda and Uganda, mountain gorillas are surviving and their numbers increasing thanks to tourism. In India, tiger populations are healthiest

---

[15] http://www.tipse.org/conscious-tourism-pdf-download/ (accessed 15 August 2017).
[16] https://destinationthink.com/destination-marketers-collaborators-dmos-net-benefit-tourism-communities/ (accessed 13 August 2017).

Fig. 4.4. Wildlife sightings at Nam Nern are scored according to rarity.

in the parks that benefit most from tourism. According to Ralf Buckley, director of the International Centre for Ecotourism Research:

> For over half of the red-listed mammal species with available data, at least 5 per cent of all wild individuals rely on tourism revenue to survive. For one in five species – including rhinos, lions and elephants – that rises to at least 15 per cent of individuals ... take it away and animals are killed by hunters. It happens every single day, every time patrols stop or hungry locals lose conservation incentives.[17]

Misool, an Indonesian dive operator and lodge, has led moves to transform an area in Raja Ampat that was previously used for illegal shark finning into a marine reserve. In just six years, since its efforts to get the practice outlawed and to support responsible diving in its place, the amount of fish has risen by 250%, and by up to 600% at some of the key dive sites. There are now 25 times more sharks found inside the Marine Reserve than directly outside, while manta ray sightings rose 25-fold over the same time period.

With coral reefs worldwide threatened by rising sea temperatures caused by global warming, Misool offers more than just a story of local success, because its

---

[17] https://www.newscientist.com/article/mg21628860-200-endangered-animals-caught-in-the-tourist-trap/ (accessed 13 August 2017).

reefs have been found to be particularly resistant to the warming seas, and thus to potentially offer a way to regenerate reefs elsewhere being destroyed by unprecedented bleaching events. According to Conservation International:

> Reefs across Raja Ampat experience temperatures fluctuating between 19 and 36 degrees Celsius (66–96 degrees Fahrenheit), with many individual reefs exposed to a whopping 6–12 C variation within a single 24-hour period! According to most marine biology textbooks, such variation should easily kill these corals, yet they are thriving.[18]

These wonderful, intricate, ecosystems are part of far more complex networks than one sees through a mask. They serve as barriers against the worst impacts of storms, protecting the beaches and the millions of people who live by them, with The Nature Conservancy reporting that 'reefs act as a speed bump for slowing storm damage, reducing up to 97 percent of a wave's energy; losing just 1 meter of reef height can lead to twice the amount of damage onshore'.[19] They are home to fish that provide food and livelihoods for nearly 100 million people. 'Coral reefs could be considered the poster child of nature-based tourism', says the Nature Conservancy, whose recent Mapping Ocean Wealth (MOW) initiative revealed that 70 million trips are supported by the world's coral reefs, representing US$36 billion a year in economic value. 'It's clear that the tourism industry depends on coral reefs. But now, more than ever, coral reefs are depending on the tourism industry', observed Dr Robert Brumbaugh, Director of Ocean Planning & Protection at The Nature Conservancy.[20]

This mutual dependency affects more than just coral reefs and those who live near them. Just as tourism can protect nature from poachers, so it needs to protect those women and men who devote their lives to doing so. Two hundred environmental activists, wildlife rangers and indigenous leaders trying to protect their lands were killed in 2016, according to the watchdog group Global Witness – more than double the number killed five years ago.[21]

CITES (The Convention on the Trade in Endangered Species) is one of the largest and oldest conservation and sustainable use agreements in existence, signed by 182 states and the European Union. At WTTC's 2017 global summit, CITES' Secretary-General John Scanlon laid out the industry's potential when it comes to conservation, and the responsibility that goes with it, stating:

---

[18] http://blog.conservation.org/2016/06/amid-widespread-coral-bleaching-this-reef-is-thriving/ (accessed 25 July 2017).

[19] https://global.nature.org/content/insuring-nature-to-ensure-a-resilient-future (accessed 25 July 2017).

[20] https://global.nature.org/content/coral-reef-tourism (accessed 25 July 2017).

[21] https://www.theguardian.com/environment/2017/jul/13/environmental-defenders-being-killed-in-record-numbers-globally-new-research-reveals (accessed 15 July 2017).

for weasels, hawks, foxes and badgers. And the carrion left behind by the wolves attracted greater numbers of bald eagles and bears.

Finally, all the new vegetation stabilized the riverbanks, protecting them from further erosion. And all of these impacts make for a more beautiful place for tourists to experience, who in turn provide funds for its protection. Initiatives such as this turn the business concepts that underpin the circular economy into inspiring narratives of restoring the natural beauty of places we love, and creating a more flourishing world for all to enjoy.

Transforming Transport 5

> Prudence never kindled a fire in the human mind; I have no hope for conservation born of fear.
>
> Aldo Leopold, *The Farmer as a Conservationist*

What is the role of transport in delivering sustainable tourism?

One of the rules of speaking on the merits of sustainable tourism at travel conferences is that when the hands go up at the end for questions, one of their arms is attached to someone who wants to ask you how flying fits into your vision of a responsible, sustainable tourism industry. And not so much as ask, as call you out for hypocrisy.

They have a point. Hotels are able to make significant progress in reducing their emissions and other impacts. Most locally based experiences' impacts are fairly negligible, depending on the forms of transport used in the destination. The other major forms of mass transport, rail and bus, are either already relatively low carbon, or are progressing fast. And while the use of cars in tourism has significant impact, the overall emissions impact is mitigated by the fact that while someone is driving a car on holiday, their own car is most probably parked up and not polluting at home. Of course using an electric car or public transport would have far greater impact, but this would apply to how they travel at home too.

The trouble is, where most other sectors are able to reduce their emissions considerably, aviation is stuck with fossil fuels for the foreseeable future, since little progress has been made in finding an alternative fuel solution. A 2016 study examined the disconnect between reporting of supposed technological solutions to aviation's environmental impacts and the reality of their development. The researchers dismissed solar-powered flying, stating that even those who had flown the Solar Impulse 2 solar-powered aircraft around the world said it will never replace the current air transport model, since 'This single-seat aircraft required enough solar cells to cover a wingspan the size of a 500-seater Boeing 747 airliner to generate enough power even to carry its single pilot aloft.'

Electric flight requires 'a 15-fold increase in the energy density of lithium batteries', and even if this were possible it wouldn't happen before 2035. And while the most efficient biofuels reduce CO_2 emissions by up to 90%, they either demand that too much agricultural land be turned over to producing fuel for a minority of people to fly, or they do not produce enough energy to make them financially viable. Technological developments continue to surprise, and a solution may be available faster than expected. But for now nothing appears on the horizon.

Meanwhile, at the end of 2016, the UN's International Civil Aviation Organization (ICAO) pledged to increase fleet fuel efficiency by 1.5% annual increments up to 2020, and aims for so-called 'carbon-neutral growth' after that, with the ultimate goal of reducing net CO_2 emissions by 50% compared with 2005 levels by 2050. The word net is the key, since the total emissions created by aviation itself will have gone up by then, whatever impact improved fuels, technology and operations have on the efficiency of the individual airplanes. The ability to claim a net reduction comes through the plan to buy enough carbon offsets to allow the industry to keep growing. In April 2017, however, a report claimed that 90% of the industry's proposed carbon offsets were not likely to provide additionality – meaning they were financing carbon reductions that would have happened anyway.

Furthermore, while the individual planes being designed are getting incrementally more efficient, the total number of planes in the sky is growing, partly because the older, less efficient planes are still flying. According to the ICAO, the global air transport network doubles in size at least once every 15 years, and will do so again by 2030. Boeing estimates that the global growth in air travel will require around 39,620 new planes over the next 20 years.

Rather than look for ways to reduce the total number of flights, however, we are building airports to provide for them. In 2016, China's population made just 138 million international trips (they made 4.44 billion domestic trips the same year). The country is planning to build 136 new airports by 2025, in total capable of transporting 2.2 billion passengers a year.[1] When Dubai's World Central Airport project opens (predicted 2018), it alone will see more than 200 million passengers a year, which is more than all five of London's airports combined.[2]

In the UK, the Tyndall Centre for Climate Change Research concludes that without swift action to curtail aviation growth, all other UK sectors will have to completely decarbonize by 2050 to compensate. This pattern can be

---

[1] http://www.globaltimes.cn/content/1038004.shtml (accessed 17 August 2017).
[2] http://www.dubaiairports.ae/corporate/media-centre/fact-sheets/detail/dubai-world-central-(dwc) (accessed 17 August 2017).

seen across the world, which is why a 2016 UN report predicts the aviation sector could consume up to 27% of the global carbon budget by 2050.

Can we justify the ongoing growth in aviation?

According to the Air Transport Action Group, 'Including direct, indirect, and induced effects, air transport supports 36 million jobs within tourism, contributing around US$892 billion a year to world GDP.'[3] It sounds like a lot, although it represents just 11.7% of tourism's total direct, indirect and induced impact of US$7.6 trillion to the global economy, and 12% of the 292 million jobs the industry supported in 2016.

One of the biggest claims for the economic importance of international tourism is that it transfers money from richer to poorer countries, and that many of these are remote island states – the Caribbean or Indian Ocean islands, for example, for whom, other than cruise ships, flying is the only viable means of bringing in significant numbers of foreign guests. In 2015, the world's 49 least developed countries (LDCs) received revenues from tourism amounting to US$21 billion.

Many of these countries also stand to suffer most from the impacts of climate change. A 2014 study by Peeters and Eijgelaar found that the economic impacts on these countries of climate mitigation policies aimed at reducing tourism air transport may be less severe than is generally supposed. On average, the impacts on LDCs were found to be 'neutral', with the maximum loss estimated at US$1.4 billion, which represents around 0.076% of the global direct GDP of tourism. At such a level, claim the authors, it would be perfectly feasible to compensate countries that lose out from a reduction in aviation-based tourism, for example through levying an additional charge on long-haul flights that could be used directly to support these countries' development.[4]

Flights are – relatively speaking – cheap because aviation pays no tax on fuel thanks to air service agreements which prohibit the imposition of tax on fuel sold for international flights. Because of this and the other subsidies it continues to receive, it is often the cheapest option. As a result, we have bought into the idea that, in the age of Ryanair etc., suddenly flying is so cheap that everyone is doing it. But less than 10% of the world's population flew on holiday last year, and most of those only flew once. Even in wealthier countries such as the UK, 15% of the population take more than 70% of the flights. As Andrew Murphy writes on the Transport and Environment website: 'This means that the most carbon-intensive mode of

---

[3] https://www.aviationbenefits.org/social-development/tourism/ (accessed 17 August 2017).
[4] https://www.tourism-watch.de/en/content/possible-impact-air-transport-restrictions (accessed 17 August 2017).

Fig. 5.1. The ground operations at Cochin's airport are the first in the world to be powered by solar.

transport, which is used most often by the wealthiest section of society, receives a massive tax exemption calculated at €60 billion a year on a global level.'[5] Because of such subsidies, write Stefan Gössling, Frank Fichert and Peter Forsyth in a 2017 paper, which seeks to assess the scope of aviation subsidies: 'there is a danger that these have overstated the economic benefits of aviation while simultaneously omitting its cost, for instance with regard to climate change'.[6]

Nonetheless, whenever there are campaigns to make aviation pay more, one of the most common retorts is that it will penalize the poor. This misrepresentation needs to be continually debunked, while also supporting moves to cost flying fairly, through schemes such as the proposed Frequent Flyer Levy. Currently, those who fly most are subsidized to do so, through loyalty schemes that offer them discounts and perks. The scheme proposes that everyone could have one tax-free flight a year, with each additional flight being taxed at an increasing level. Research by the New Economics Foundation (NEF) found that such a levy would make it unnecessary to build any new runways in the UK, while making everyone's first flight more affordable. According to NEF, 'a progressive tax on frequent flying could play a significant role in restraining demand for flights, while at the same time tending to distribute those flights more equally across the income spectrum'.[7]

---

[5] https://www.transportenvironment.org/newsroom/blog/see-how-reformed-aviation-ets-can-work-better (accessed 27 June 2017).

[6] http://www.mdpi.com/2071-1050/9/8/1295/htm (accessed 17 August 2017).

[7] https://s3-eu-west-1.amazonaws.com/media.afreeride.org/documents/FFL+Modelling+paper.pdf (accessed 17 August 2017).

If your business model relies on guests flying, then you need to factor that into any assessment of your impacts. Many of the world's airports are combining facilitating aviation's ongoing growth with an increased focus on greening their own operations. India's Cochin Airport is now the world's first fully solar-powered airport, while others are now buying enough off-sets to declare themselves carbon neutral. Some are attempting to redesign according to circular principles, notably Schipol (a member of the Circular Economy 100), and Gatwick and Heathrow, both of whose bids for the UK's next runway draw heavily on the circular economy in their design. 'Let's not lose sight of the fact that Gatwick's commitment extends only to the airport infrastructure and vehicles', commented Deputy Director of the Aviation Environment Federation, Cait Hewitt. 'The planes that fly out of Gatwick are still powered by fossil fuels and will remain so for decades to come. Around 99% of the emissions associated with Gatwick are not from the airport itself but from the aircraft that use it.'[8]

Destinations also ignore the impacts of the tourists that their international marketing seeks to attract. Professor Xavier Font, who has recently authored a new 2020 Tourism Strategy for Barcelona, writes:

> Destinations must also be accountable for the transport impact of their visitors. The marketing department might prefer a Japanese tourist to Barcelona because on average they will spend €40 more than a French tourist – according to unpublished data from the Barcelona Tourist Board – but the carbon footprint we collectively pay for is not taken into account.[9]

Hotels and international tour companies also rarely consider it their responsibility, regardless of how much of their marketing is focussed internationally, in part because the flights are more often booked independently by the traveller. As mentioned earlier, Soneva Fushi is one of the few exceptions in terms of hotels. Among tour operators, Better Places offsets all the carbon emissions from its clients' trips – both the in destination component and the flights – despite not selling flights itself. It invests that money in more efficient cooking stoves in Ghana.

When it comes to the tourists themselves, it's clear from the ongoing growth in overall numbers of people flying by air that few tourists are cutting back either. 'One of the reasons sustainability lacks appeal is it's described as a down concept', writes George Lakoff in *Metaphors We Live By*. 'We're asked to reduce our emissions or live a low-impact lifestyle ... Refusing to fly takes this heresy to its extreme: here is someone literally renouncing the high-life.'

Of course people want to fly. We have been bombarded with seductive imagery about the freedom it gives us. However, a combination of factors

---

[8] http://www.aef.org.uk/2017/01/18/gatwicks-carbon-neutral-commitment-excludes-99-of-emissions/ (accessed 17 August 2017).
[9] https://theconversation.com/how-to-stop-city-breaks-killing-our-cities-79132 (accessed 27 July 2017).

conspire to make our perception and experience of travelling by air considerably worse than its romantic presentation. Security concerns and financial pressures are making the experience less pleasurable. And climate change is set to make the flight even more so. According to a 2017 study:

> light turbulence will increase by 59%, and light-to-moderate turbulence will increase by 75%. In other words, expect more spilled drinks and dire warning to buckle up. Things get worse from there, with the incidence of increasingly severe turbulence going up, up, and up. Truly severe turbulence – jolts harsh enough to toss people around – will climb 149%.[10]

How can tourism support more sustainable alternatives?

Inbound companies need to make it as easy as possible for visitors to reach them by public transport. The International Union of Railways has recently launched TopRail to raise awareness of cruise and heritage railways, and scenic train routes around the world. Currently, just 2% of international tourism uses the rail networks, yet according to Vanessa Pérez, TopRail project manager, 'Supporting sustainable tourism using railways is not only a strategic framework for ensuring a positive image of railways, but also a way to answer to social concerns, create a competitive advantage and manage risk.'[11]

Because it can be challenging for visitors to work out how they might reach a location by train or coach, hotel and destination websites can help by providing more information about journey times, how best to make connections, and any additional advice for tourists travelling with luggage in places they don't know and where they may not speak the language. Seat61.com has done a remarkable job of analysing the world's railway routes, and although it is weighted towards journeys from the UK, this information is easily adaptable to journeys starting elsewhere. Likewise, loco2.com sells tickets for journeys across Europe and is an official agent for rail operators in the UK, France, Spain, Italy and Germany.

Greentraveller.co.uk was founded by Richard Hammond, with whom I co-wrote the guidebook *Clean Breaks* in 2010. It promotes holidays that are accessible without flying from the UK, and provides detailed guidance on how to get there, how long it takes and, by working with ecopassenger.com, information on what the carbon emissions resulting from the trip are.

Websites offering trips and holidays could be structured so as to prioritize options that a tourist could reach without flying. Bookdifferent.com has tried a similar approach with hotels, where a search for a destination returns

---

[10] https://link.springer.com/article/10.1007/s00376-017-6268-2 (accessed 27 July 2017).
[11] http://www.railway-technology.com/features/featuretoprail-promoting-sustainable-rail-tourism-5852451/ (accessed 11 July 2017).

the most sustainable options at the top of a set of results. At the Dolphin Hotel on the remote Irish island of Inishbofin, their How to Get To Us page makes no mention of airports. Instead they lay out the options for ferry, train, bus and bike.[12]

Snowcarbon focuses exclusively on how to go skiing in Europe without flying. A few ski companies also promote rail, with large operators Crystal and Inghams offering rail packages at the same price as the alternative by air. The Hidden Alps chalet group offers a discount for anyone arriving by rail. However, rail booking systems don't help this develop further, because many rail journeys to the Alps go on sale only 2–3 months in advance, yet most people want to book their holidays a year ahead.

Very few companies consider accessibility issues relating to low carbon alternatives when it comes to the transport advice they provide. Sites like wheelchairtravel.org provide information on how well a range of popular destinations care for people with accessibility needs with their public transport, but I am yet to see this sort of information incorporated into most hotel and tour company literature. Hotels and tour companies should work with local and international experts to ensure they provide the best access information to help guests reach them. In 2017, Accomable, a global platform for accessible hotels and holiday rentals, partnered with the EU-funded EuTravel Project to find ways to make it possible to book door-to-door accessible transport across the EU via a single platform.[13]

As well as publicly supporting such schemes and informing their customers, there are many ways to further encourage lower carbon transport. In South Africa, many of the camps and lodges offered by Transfrontier Parks Destinations are sold at a considerable discount to tourists from Southern Africa. The primary reason is to encourage locals to get to know their own country better, but such differential pricing can also reduce the number of flights taken. It may also boost occupancy in the long run, as people are more likely to return to places that they can access easily, and tell their friends who can also do so.

Destinations can also support low-carbon options. Werfenweng is a small alpine village that is committed to promoting car-free tourism. Guests who arrive by train and those who hand over their car keys on arrival are issued with a mobility-guarantee card giving them access to free electric transport around the region. As a result, train arrivals are up 20%. Likewise the Swiss cities Basel and Geneva both offer free public transport to all tourists so that they can use their hotel reservations as a ticket from their airport

---

[12] http://www.dolphinhotel.ie/ecotourism/green-travel-carbon-offsetting/ (accessed 19 June 2017).
[13] https://www.ttgmedia.com/news/technology/accomable-signs-up-to-eutravel-project-11261 (accessed 20 August 2017).

Fig. 5.2. How Werfenweng's mobility guarantee card works.

(or international rail station) to the hotel, where they receive an unlimited travel pass for the city and the region.[14]

Tourism companies can realign their own internal practices to support greater uses of more sustainable forms of transport, for example by making it easier for their own staff to holiday without flying. Futerra is a communication agency working with companies to improve their sustainability messaging. Its co-founder Ed Gillespie wrote a book recounting a year's travel round the world without flying, while one of its clients is Heathrow, with whom it is working on a new sustainability vision. Futerra's staff are given an extra day's paid holiday if they choose to go on holiday by means other than plane.

None of these approaches have been discussed much, although a new European scheme is at least exploring what might be possible. In 2016, the European Parliament debated whether all young Europeans should be given a free Interrail pass when they turned 18. Although it was rejected, its replacement is as interesting, because it has been structured to make tourism more sustainable, more available to those from a more disadvantaged background, and to support the destinations people visit.

Under the new scheme, school children will discuss travel plans in class, knowing they will be selected on the 'extent to which social inclusion (e.g. of disadvantaged young people) has been taken into account in their project and whether the class has travelled abroad before'. The trips they propose have to meet two further criteria, one on carbon emissions, and the other encouraging longer stays. They will have to calculate the carbon intensiveness of their itinerary using a system that favours more sustainable forms of transport and which means that no trip that is exclusively by air (or small ferry) will be possible.

---

[14] https://www.congress.ch/-/media/congress/Documents/PressReleases/2016/research-free-public-transport.pdf (accessed 20 August 2017).

While it will still be feasible for the children to include air travel in their plans, they will have to include overland travel, probably by train. Finally the ratio between the time spent travelling and the time at destination should not exceed 1 day travelling to 4 days in a destination. By promoting shorter journeys and longer stays the scheme is encouraging students to visit and get to understand their neighbours better, rather than jet off a long way away for a quick fix of the exotic. They can go further, but they will have to stay longer to justify it.

* * *

Because hotels employ offsetting, I looked at the mechanisms in chapter 2. However, offsetting is more often associated with flying, which accounts for the vast majority of a trip's emissions. I studied the websites of four of the best known international responsible tourism operators, who each offer a significant number of trips that necessitate flying. Each one of them had a different approach to offsetting. One provided links for tourists wanting to offset. One explained how they have offset all the on-trip costs themselves, and that the cost is included in the price. One explicitly rejected offsets as a distraction. And one made no mention of them at all.

This sends very mixed messages to concerned travellers. The issue remains controversial, but I see little sign that the industry is working together to resolve any contradictions. As I stated in Chapter 2, I consider that the correct approach is to use offsets, but only as the final stage in the widely accepted mitigation hierarchy: Avoid, Minimize, Offset. I consider it the correct approach because efforts to vilify carbon offsets have resulted in less carbon offsetting (and so less money to support vital sustainability and community initiatives), but not less flying.

And I think we should all pay for them. Every tourist should pay to offset their flight. Every airline should pay for every flight someone takes on one of their planes. Every destination should pay for every flight that lands at its airport. Every tour company for every flight it designs into the tours it sells. And every hotel for every international guest that stays. International travel could raise billions to support eco entrepreneurship and carbon sequestration around the world.

Of course, it wouldn't be that simple, because all that would happen is the tourist would pay for their offsets five times, as all the others would pass the price on. So how about a model rather like when companies offer to match donations by their staff to charities? Only after I have agreed the price for my flight am I offered the chance to offset it, knowing that the airline will match my contribution.

Whatever one thinks of offsetting, the carbon pricing it represents will be ubiquitous in international tourism when the aviation industry includes it in its growth strategy from 2020, and when the price of everyone's tickets will go up. It won't just be aviation that is affected by the eventual adoption of carbon pricing mechanisms. According to Sustainable Brands, 60% of the world's 500 largest asset owners, worth US$27 trillion, recognize the financial risks of climate change, and in 2017 Australia's Commonwealth Bank (CommBank) became the first business to be sued by shareholders for not properly disclosing the risks posed to its business by climate change.[15] Already banks such as HSBC and BNP Paribas are investigating how they can use carbon pricing to address climate risk in their portfolios. Cote d'Ivoire is seeing how it might tackle poverty while enabling the African country to meet its climate target, and China is launching a national Emissions Trading System.

In May 2017, the World Bank released a report into carbon pricing and the latest innovations driving its adoption, which concluded that a carbon price of US$40–80 per ton of CO_2 equivalent by 2020, rising to US$50–100 per ton by 2030, when combined with supportive policies such as public transport investment, renewable power, urban planning and forest protection, would allow for achievement of the Paris goal.[16] 'Climate change has been a growing crisis for decades, and we're running out of time', said the World Bank's president Jim Yong Kim on the release of the report. 'I hope that by sharing these success stories, we can inspire others to discover their own solutions and move with the speed and scale we need to finally address climate change.'

---

[15] http://www.sustainablebrands.com/news_and_views/marketing_comms/sustainable_brands/first-ever_lawsuit_over_indequate%E2%80%99_climate_risk_di (accessed 17 August 2017).
[16] http://www.worldbank.org/en/news/press-release/2017/05/29/new-global-pathway-on-carbon-pricing-can-shift-finance-to-sustainable-investments-world-bank (accessed 17 August 2017).

Transforming Communication

6

I can only answer the question, 'What am I to do?' if I can answer the prior question, 'Of what story or stories do I find myself a part?'

Alasdair McIntyre, *After Virtue*

Everywhere you look, a certain type of tourist – always not our travelling selves – is being blamed for damage happening to the world. Some look down on those who go on vast cruise ships. Others shake their heads at drunken youth. Or ridicule newly affluent tourists for their rookie mistakes.

Of course, individual tourists can behave more responsibly. But the main problem with tourism is not the individual who acts inappropriately. It is the system that channels unmanageable numbers of tourists into a limited number of fragile places.

The growth of the industry has been built on promoting the low hanging fruit. Venice is easy to excite people about – it's got canals instead of streets. Elephants don't need a PR campaign to make us think they are incredible.

We've been pummelled into believing it takes a long flight to find the elixir of holiday calm. A transformative approach to tourism could ease the pressure by helping people to experience a sense of wonder anywhere, anytime. As Marcus Aurelius wrote in the 2nd Century:

> Let it be clear to you that the peace of green fields can always be yours in this, that, or any other spot; and that nothing is any different here from what it would be either up in the hills, or down by the sea, or wherever else you will.

Tourism marketing encourages us to perceive our holiday as a subset of work. It is no more than 'time off'. We work to afford the holiday and the conspicuous consumption that demands. We holiday in order to restore ourselves to return to work. This diminishes the value of time spent not working. 'Leisure is not a respite from effortful work', write Ilan Stavans and Joshua Ellison in *Reclaiming Travel*.[1] 'Leisure is an encounter with the intrinsically good, the fundamentally and definitely human.'

---

[1] Ilan Stevans and Joshua Ellison (2015) *Reclaiming Travel*, p. 78.

When we go on holiday many of us seek out the habits and habitats of a place we may never return to. We seek to connect, and to understand. But rarely do we do this at home. 'We rush after what is remote and remain indifferent to what is nearby', wrote another Roman author, Pliny.

This rush for the remote is enabled by the aviation industry's unsustainable growth model. But tourism is not aviation, and it doesn't have to model its progress on it. Of course there will still be international tourism, and people will continue to fly around the world so long as there is fuel to power the planes. But transformative tourism has to be about more than just giving people more engaging experiences when they get out of the airport. It has to be about bringing tourism back down to earth and into people's daily lives. As Jost Krippendorf wrote in *The Holiday Makers*, the challenge is 'to make that which is felt to be the counter-world a natural part of social reality, to have in short more holiday in everyday life'.[2]

Having launched in London in 2015, a social enterprise called Street Wisdom is now hosting urban walks in 27 countries. It describes itself as 'a global social enterprise with a mission to bring inspiration to every street on earth'. It takes people on three-hour exploratory walks around streets near where they live. Through a series of thought exercises and suggestions from the guide, it helps participants see the world around them with fresh eyes – even if it is just the street round the corner from their flat. 'Why wait for escape to exotic destinations', asks Street Wisdom's website, 'when inspiration can be found on your own doorstep?'

In the late spring of 2017, I spent three revelatory hours a few miles from my own front door, on an urban foraging tour with Robin Harford, creator of the UK's leading wild food site, Eatweeds. I was introduced to – and tasted – countless plant species that grow near me. I left asking myself why I don't do things like this more often. Why I only tend to see the world with the wide-eyed excitement of a tourist when I have taken a week off to go on holiday, somewhere else. Why I can identify more bird species in South Africa than in the UK.

Using tourism to bring people closer to the biodiversity or culture on their own doorstep enriches their everyday life. It makes them more excited about what is happening around them. Because they are nearby, they are more likely to return. And as people gain greater awareness of their own local environments and their specific conservation issues, they are more likely to support or engage in efforts to protect and restore them. As Robin Harford told me during our walk, it helps us to 'know our place in the world'.

I could highlight how any number of other local experiences in this book have deepened my understanding of where I live, from the rewilding safari at Knepp to the Unseen tour of London's streets with a homeless guide. What sets the experience with Eatweeds apart, however, was the communication before and after. In the weeks leading up to the walk I received emails from Harford about wild plants, introducing me to ideas, stories,

---

[2] Jost Krippendorf (1999) *The Holiday Makers*, p. 77.

videos that might enrich my experience, either on the day or afterwards. Following on from the day of the tour, he continued to send more information, deepening a curiosity that began with an experience a few hours one Sunday, and which as a result I can't wait to experience again.

Rather than bombarding them with discounts and offers for far-off places, companies' communication with their customers can share stories and information about the issues that defined their time, becoming a part of their life not as yet another inbox marketeer, but as a provider of insight and inspiration. I'm never going to share a special offer with my friends on social media. But send me a story about an issue I care about, and I might post it and so do a company's marketing for them.

How can social media transform tourism?

When I set off to write a guidebook in 2007, TripAdvisor was seven years old. Facebook was three, YouTube two. The iPhone was invented that year, revolutionizing the way travellers record and share their experiences. Instagram, Snapchat and Pinterest did not yet exist. In 2007, most photos were taken for personal consumption. Information on places and experiences was gained from a limited range of authors, journalists and the marketing of the destination marketing organizations.

By 2015, there were more than 53 million candid traveller photos on TripAdvisor, with 200 new user contributions to the site every minute. Some 300 million new photos are added to Facebook each day. According to travel technology website Tnooz, the most shared content on social networking sites are holiday photos and in 2012, 42% of stories shared by Facebook users were about their travel experiences. Today, one out of three American travellers say social networking sites are their main source of ideas when planning holidays.

In 2017, following campaigns maintained and magnified by people sharing photos and stories on social media, both TripAdvisor and Expedia (along with several tour companies) committed to stop selling certain types of experiences that involved animal interactions. They are both now working with conservation and animal welfare organizations to create information portals to educate their users on such issues. And in July 2016, Tinder's CEO called on the dating app's users to stop posting tiger selfies to their profiles.

Looking for uses beyond influencing tourists in their holiday planning, researchers are exploring how to utilize this vast and ever-growing repository of user-generated travel data to transform the world. The Nature Conservancy is creating the online Atlas of Ocean Wealth by combining traditional data-driven academic research with crowd-sourced and social media-related data to assess the economic contribution of coral reefs in different countries, and thus provide incentives for their protection. By mapping hotel locations alongside the number of photos taken in a location, and measuring and comparing photos of dive-sites and underwater photographs versus tourism activities that indirectly benefit from the presence of

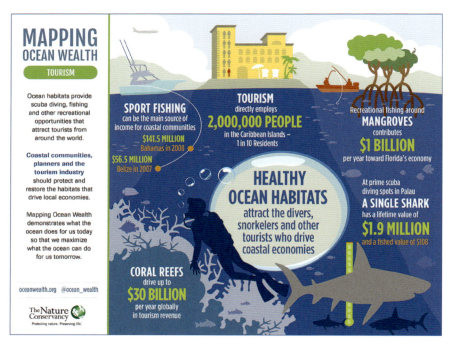

Fig. 6.1. The Nature Conservancy's Mapping Ocean Wealth initiative seeks to cost the ecosystem services provided by the ocean.

coral reefs, researchers have created far more precise assessments of value than previously possible. They are now developing an innovative insurance programme called the Reef Resilience Fund where hotels whose businesses benefit from the presence of nearby reefs will pay the premiums for their protection and restoration in the event of storm damage.

In Australia, Griffith University is analysing Twitter to measure the health of the Great Barrier Reef. Researchers downloaded almost 300,000 tweets posted from the Great Barrier Reef between July 2016 and March 2017. They selected 13,344 potentially useful tweets by filtering for relevant keywords such as 'fish', 'coral', 'turtle' or 'bleach'. Of these tweets, 61% had geographic coordinates that enabled the researchers to plot their location and attribute their opinions to conditions on specific areas of reef. Although the research is still in its early stages, this meant researchers were able to pick out patterns such as concern over the welfare of dugongs.[3]

Launched in 2016, TraffickCam is a free mobile app that enables anyone staying in a hotel room to anonymously share a photograph of it to a central database. Because sex traffickers often post images of their victims posed in

---

[3] https://theconversation.com/tweet-streams-how-social-media-can-help-keep-tabs-on-ecosystems-health-82368 (accessed 18 August 2017).

hotel rooms for online advertisements, TraffickCam is able to match patterns in the carpeting, furniture, room accessories and window views from such adverts against the database of traveller images and provide law enforcement with a list of potential hotels where the photo may have been taken.

The ever-growing volume of data being produced and shared on social media, combined with the ubiquity of cameraphones and the rapid development of digital initiatives such as Blockchain, should be seen as a revolution in transparency that supports efforts towards a more responsible, sustainable tourism supply chain. If we ignore it, then we are treating the insights it contains as disposable waste rather than seeing how we can factor them back in to improve the system. Organizations like Made By, Provenance and HowGood are making supply chain ethics and sustainability data instantly accessible to consumers and companies. Platforms like Bafin are making it easier for whistle-blowers to expose labour rights abuses anonymously. The Greek island of Agistri has experimented with a Blockchain-enabled cryptocurrency called Drachmae that would enable tourists and travel businesses to circumvent the collapse of Greece's traditional economy and continue to transact with confidence while on the island, while also addressing challenges of economic leakage by keeping the money circulating locally.[4]

Anyone working for a more sustainable tourism industry should tap into and encourage such shifts toward more positive, responsible communication. The potential to positively influence both tourist and company behaviour is huge.

How can communication support transformative tourism?

There are several organizations, publications and websites looking to share stories of best practice and support further communication and collaboration. The International Tourism Partnership and its editorial website Greenhotelier work with major hotel groups, with a particular focus on issues around carbon, water, human rights and youth employment. The Long Run Initiative brings together many of the world's leading safari and conservation-focused tourism organizations. New York-based Impact Travel Alliance is developing an international network of city-based hubs to help tourism media professionals and entrepreneurs collaborate with one another. And the organizers of mainstream travel trade events such as WTM, ITB, WTTC and PATA all have initiatives from seminars and award programmes to dedicated responsible tourism networking events.

All tourism is a form of communication, because it is dialogue between a place and its inhabitants and those who come to visit. It is stories and experiences, memories and encounters. This is most obvious in the case of

---

[4] http://news.wtm.com/airbnb-blockchain-and-the-tourism-reputation-economy/ (accessed 18 August 2017).

many of the tour companies I have profiled, such as Mejdi Tours introducing tourists to differing stories and perspectives around regions of conflict, or Migrantours giving European immigrants the chance to share their ways of seeing and living in a city.

By effectively managing guest expectations and knowledge in advance of their arrival (or booking), tourism communication can look to improve interactions between visitors and residents, hopefully making for a more re-warding time for both. Viaggi Solidali, which is involved with running the Migrantours initiatives, uses walking tours within migrant communities in participants' home cities as a form of 'pre-trip communication' introducing travellers to aspects of the cultures they are considering visiting.

Transformative tourism should communicate how it is possible to com-bine a better guest experience with positive impacts on the world. Nam Nern's safari points system shows how fighting poaching means improved safari viewing. Martin's Eco-Bon loyalty scheme rewards guests for sustain-able behaviour. Guldsmeden connects its efforts to attain organic food cer-tification with its ability to focus more on its guests. UK bed and breakfast Beechenhill Farm's website says:

> Because we have made green choices you will have a better time: our biomass boiler is providing heat and lashings of hot water at any time of day or night, so you'll be cosy and warm and our induction hobs cook quickly and efficiently so you will spend less time in the kitchen.

Such communication can engage guests in a company's efforts by clearly demonstrating how their choices make a difference. This might be Radisson Blu's towel strategy explicitly quantifying the number of reused towels needed to provide one child with drinking water for life or the Economic Nutrition Labelling featured on Fogo Island Inn's bills.

All of the above, and many other approaches featured in this book, should be seen as parts of a wider shift away from the negative and con-fused framing that has typified much sustainability communication. This is exemplified by the perception that we are in a 'war against carbon', and the way that the descriptions 'carbon negative' and 'carbon positive' are used interchangeably to mean the same thing.

In 2016, Bill McDonough, co-founder of Cradle to Cradle and inaugural Chair of the World Economic Forum's Meta-Council on Circular Economy, called for a rethink in the way we talk about climate change. His proposal for a New Language of Carbon reimagines sustainability communication in the same way that Project Drawdown looks at climate solutions, the circular economy re-designs business, and that I have approached transforming tourism in this book.

'Our goal is simple and positive', writes McDonough. 'A delightfully diverse, safe, healthy and just world – with clean air, soil, water and energy – economically, equitably, ecologically and elegantly enjoyed.'[5]

---

[5] https://www.nature.com/news/carbon-is-not-the-enemy-1.20976 (accessed 17 August 2017).

Conclusion: Transforming Tourism

7

I wouldn't give a fig for the simplicity on this side of complexity; I would give my right arm for the simplicity on the far side of complexity.

Oliver Wendell Holmes

Can the mainstream be transformed?

This book has explored what truly transformative tourism might look like, highlighting many of the most impactful examples out there. There are several I have only briefly mentioned, and even more that I have not featured, due to limitations of space. I have tried to illustrate as wide a range of approaches as possible and have offered examples that could be part of a transformative framework. However, I have not looked in depth at the industry's mainstream, in particular the all-inclusives and cruise ships that define much of its impact. The only exception to this was aviation, because it is used by all forms of international tourism.

There are numerous individual cases of innovative sustainable design, architecture and engineering described in Chapter 2 being implemented by hotels owned by multinational chains. These same chains, along with international tour companies, could support the kind of transformative tours and experiences that are outlined in Chapter 3.

As Chapter 4 makes clear, however, the policies that make for sustainable places are mostly in the control of regional and national governments. The tourism industry can support them, can lobby in favour of more sustainable policies, but in most cases its structure is not designed to make this happen.

Take, for example, taxation. According to the author of *Sustainable Tourism on A Finite Planet*, Megan Epler Wood, 'There is little information worldwide, from any nation, on the uses of tourism taxes.' Epler Wood singles out the work of Linda Ambrosie as the one case of study in this area, through her 2016 book *Sun & Sea Tourism: Fantasy and Finance of the All-Inclusive Industry*, which reveals that due to complex structures of the world's largest all-inclusive hotel groups – where they often own the airline, the hotel, the tour companies and more besides – as little as 20% of the money that a tourist pays for an all-inclusive holiday may end up remaining in the place they visit.

Ambrosie writes:

> The system works like this. The destination-located hotel invoices the international reservation company in a tax haven such as Curaçao less than the full value of the tourists' package. The hotel shows a loss at the destination and therefore pays no taxes. The profits stay in Curaçao. When a hotel wants to expand, they bring in the untaxed profits as foreign direct investment and often even receive subsidies.[1]

There are times when economies of scale matter, and one of them is in providing enough strength to be listened to by government. Major international hotel chains, tour companies and perhaps collective bodies representing smaller hotel companies, are better placed to make their influence felt. Yet according to the report into tax in Jamaica,

> One aspect of tourism used for development, that has not been fully explored, nor attempted to get the tax policy to be consistent with that, is where incentives are provided to hotels for imports. As an hotelier, it is easier to import a bed with zero duty and zero GCT than to buy the same bed from a local manufacturer as that would require paying all the duties the manufacturer would have paid.[2]

As Ambrosie writes, when it comes to lobbying governments,

> While individuals and small companies have few means to avoid taxes, large corporations with their complex webs of companies and transfer pricing have many means at their disposal. Indirect taxes such as lodging taxes, VAT and airport taxes are collected locally. These are much harder to avoid and constitute most of the taxes that resorts pay. Destinations must seek to impose indirect taxes to ensure that the monies needed to fund environmental protection and social development remain in that locality.

Can the mainstream go circular?

The key principles that this book seeks to articulate – adopting a circular approach; looking to be a regenerative, transformative force rather than simply incrementally less negative; shifting from a model based on increasing industrial productivity to one based on promoting human flourishing and wellbeing; and a central narrative that employs transparency and honest

---

[1] https://www.tourism-watch.de/node/2517 (accessed 21 June 2017).
[2] http://www.caribbeanhotelandtourism.com/downloads/TEOxford-Travel TourismJamaica032112.pdf (accessed 21 June 2017).

storytelling to deliver a tourism experience grounded in truth – are all as accessible to large companies as to small.

On the other hand, should there be situations where the size of an operation makes such approaches impractical or unattainable, then here is where I consider that a shift in understanding needs to be made. Too often inspiring local, small-scale initiatives are undervalued for being unscaleable, implying that the ability to grow is the prerequisite of success.

The question should not be 'Is it scaleable?' but rather 'Is it replicable?' Or 'Is it adaptable?' 'Can I apply what has been implemented here somewhere else?' And even if the answer sometimes is no, then just as one looks at the project to ask why not, one should also look at how we are seeking to replicate it and ask if we are perhaps trying to do something that is too large.

Soel Yachts won a WTTC award for innovation in 2017 for developing a system of solar panels that cover the entire roof of a small vessel. When the boat is back in harbour, it can be plugged into the resort's mains supply and act as a solar array, boosting the resort's energy needs with clean, renewable energy. But I doubt it would be possible to power a giant cruise ship the same way, and even if it was, it would do nothing to address the other problems these ships cause with overtourism and waste. This should not be seen as a limitation of Soel's innovation, but a critical comment on the unsustainable size cruise ships have become and the model of tourism growth they support.

Tourism cannot be measured by standard models

The standard measurement for the economy is GDP/GNP. As the economy grows, GNP goes up. However, criticisms of GNP have been around for as long as GNP itself. As then presidential candidate Bobby Kennedy said in 1968:

> Gross National Product counts air pollution and cigarette advertising, and ambulances to clear our highways of carnage. It counts special locks for our doors and the jails for the people who break them. It counts the destruction of the redwood and the loss of our natural wonder in chaotic sprawl. It counts napalm and counts nuclear warheads and armored cars for the police to fight the riots in our cities. It counts Whitman's rifle and Speck's knife, and the television programs which glorify violence in order to sell toys to our children. Yet the gross national product does not allow for the health of our children, the quality of their education or the joy of their play. It does not include the beauty of our poetry or the strength of our marriages, the intelligence of our public debate or the integrity of our public officials. It measures neither our wit nor our courage, neither our wisdom nor our learning, neither our compassion nor our devotion to our country, it measures everything in short, except that which makes life worthwhile.[3]

---

[3] https://www.jfklibrary.org/Research/Research-Aids/Ready-Reference/RFK-Speeches/Remarks-of-Robert-F-Kennedy-at-the-University-of-Kansas-March-18-1968.aspx (accessed 21 June 2017).

Such limitations make it a particularly inappropriate measure for tourism, since most of the qualitative measures that define a good holiday are not counted. A forest adds nothing to GNP while it stands, absorbing CO_2 and providing a place where biodiversity thrives and people can walk and relax. Chop it down and sell the wood, and GNP goes up. To try to define tourism's importance by highlighting its contribution to GNP is to miss what may well be its most important contributions to the wellbeing of our societies.

From 2004 to 2012, Japan invested around US$4 million studying the physiological and psychological effects of people spending time in healthy forests, what they call 'shinrin-yoku' or 'Forest Bathing'. According to the World Economic Forum, the researchers found that such activities 'lower heart rate and blood pressure, reduce stress hormone production, boost the immune system, and improve overall feelings of wellbeing'. It's now part of the country's national health programme.

In 2017 Friends of the Earth Europe and the Institute for European Environmental Policy published the first report to draw together the evidence connecting access to nature with human health, with some astounding findings. People living over 1 kilometre from green space are more likely to be obese than those living closer than 300 metres. Doctors prescribe fewer antidepressants in urban areas with more trees on the streets. Access to nature can reduce childhood behavioural problems, such as hyperactivity, emotional symptoms and peer relationship problems. These figures are not part of a GNP/GDP-focused interpretation of tourism benefits, yet they should be central to a future narrative based on transformation.

The Economics of Ecosystems and Biodiversity (TEEB) is an international initiative to draw attention to the global benefits of biodiversity, such as how 15% of worldwide CO_2 emissions are absorbed by forests every year. Starting in 2008, it has attempted to cost the value of the 'ecosystem services' provided by the natural world, highlighting both the costs incurred from their loss or destruction and the benefits they offer while sustained and nurtured. While ideally we would appreciate the intrinsic value of nature and not need such a mechanism to justify preservation, TEEB's findings are significant.

For an annual investment of US$45 billion into protected areas alone, the delivery of ecosystem services worth some US$5 trillion a year could be secured. A 2012 report by TEEB highlighted how

> investments in protected areas have led to benefits in a number of countries, including increased visitor spending in protected areas in Finland, low cost water supply to the city of Dunedin in New Zealand, and avoided soil erosion and improved water supply for farmers in Venezuela.

It also showed how restoration of mangroves helped with flood and storm defences in Vietnam, restoration of German peatlands helped with carbon storage and restoration of watersheds increased clean water provision to New York. As the Finnish example explicitly states, and the restoration examples imply, many of these initiatives can bring benefits to tourism through improved experiences, just as tourism can support them through increased investment, such as the 3.7 million acres of land and sea that National Geographic says the members of its Unique Lodges Collection have rehabilitated and protected since 2015.

Numerous alternative measures have been proposed to GDP, with even the World Economic Forum having a section of its website dedicated to 'Beyond GDP' which asks:

> Is our love-affair with GDP coming to an end? As the business landscape reinvents itself, demographics shift, inequality expands, climate change gets worse and technology continues to advance at breakneck speed, Gross Domestic Product is struggling to stay relevant. In order to keep up with the changes wrought by the Fourth Industrial Revolution, many are arguing that we need to find a new measure to assess the health of our economies and – more importantly – the people living in them.[4]

One of the best known of these new measures is GNH, or Gross National Happiness. In 1972, the landlocked Himalayan country of Bhutan's fourth king, Jigme Singye Wangchuck, declared his country would seek development through policies designed to increase happiness rather than simply growth in productivity. While such a singular proclamation may seem the act of a benign dictator, the same king also drafted a constitution that would entail him voluntarily renouncing power, while also protecting the present as well as the future well-being of the people and the country. In 2008, the country held its first democratic elections.

The constitution commits Bhutan to maintaining 62% of the country under forest cover, which currently stands at 72%. As a result the country claims it is carbon neutral, and will be carbon positive in a few years. Along with the forest cover, it has the world's highest proportion of land in protected areas, at 42.7%.

According to Antonia Gawel, who has worked in Bhutan as an adviser to the multilateral development banks on environmental and clean energy policy,

> What stood out however as a unique attribute of the people I met in Bhutan is the importance they place on 'time' – taking time to think, time with family, time to breathe; a recognition of time and experience past by previous generations, and the importance of future generational equity.[5]

Elsewhere, the Economy for the Common Good (ECG) is a new social movement advocating an alternative economic model, one that favours cooperation instead of profit-orientation and competition. Founded

---

[4] https://www.weforum.org/focus/beyond-gdp (accessed 21 June 2017).
[5] https://www.weforum.org/agenda/2016/05/4-lessons-from-bhutan-on-the-pursuit-of-happiness-above-gdp (accessed 21 June 2017).

by Christian Felber in 2010, it is being adopted by companies and municipalities around the world, with the state parliament of South Tyrol resolving that ECG organisations will be given priority in public contracts, and Stuttgart applying its Common Good balance sheet to four of its local services. There are a few tourism companies among over 2000 organisations that have signed up – in Italy both the Drumlerhof Hotel and Hotel La Perla are using its models as the benchmarks by which to track their own success.

Tourism could transform thinking across society by ceasing to use GDP as its headline measure. Through the widespread adoption instead of measures such as the Economy for the Common Good it could provoke discussion on what is real value, and could challenge the industry and others to rethink what defines progress.

How can tourism prepare for new work patterns?

In February 2017, computer scientist Moshe Vardi estimated that increasing automation means 50% of the world could be unemployed within 30 years.[6] Research by PricewaterhouseCoopers in 2017 reckoned 30% of jobs in the UK, 38% in the USA and 35% in Germany could be at high risk from automation by the early 2030s. In his farewell address of January 2017, President Barack Obama stated: 'The next wave of economic dislocations won't come from overseas. It will come from the relentless pace of automation that makes a lot of good, middle-class jobs obsolete.'[7]

In his 2017 book *Utopia for Realists*, Rutger Bregman explores how such changes will affect the world of work, and by association the increased amount of time available for leisure. 'Swimming in a sea of spare time will not be easy', he writes. 'A Twenty-First Century education should prepare people not only for joining the workforce, but also (and more importantly) for life.' This should be seen as a rallying call to tourism, since it is above all else the industry designed to fill up the time we have available when we aren't working. How will it respond?

Even if Finland's experiments with the Universal Income (also explored at depth in Bregman's book) become more widely implemented, if people are working less then they won't be earning more, and so the focus cannot be on selling them highly expensive holidays to be enjoyed in compressed periods of time. Regardless of what form of carbon pricing is in place, someone with several more weeks of time available but reduced money to spend, or someone who is now only working a three-day week, is considerably less

---

[6] http://www.telegraph.co.uk/news/science/science-news/12155808/Robots-will-take-over-most-jobs-within-30-years-experts-warn.html (accessed 31 May 2017).
[7] https://workingnation.com/president-obama-next-wave-economic-dislocations-will-come-automation/ (accessed 31 May 2017).

likely to blow a sizeable chunk of it on flying halfway round the world to stay in an exorbitantly priced hotel. They are more likely to be enjoying lots of the sort of compact 'microadventures' espoused by Alastair Humphries in his 2014 book of the same name, designed to 'offer a realistic escape to wilderness, simplicity and the great outdoors, without the need to ski to the South Pole or go live in a cabin in Patagonia'.[8]

Tourism needs to prepare its response, but it certainly shouldn't be a future to fear. When American scientists surveyed employees to find out whether they would rather have two weeks additional salary or two weeks off, twice as many people opted for the extra time. Likewise, countries with shorter work weeks are also those that appear at the top of gender equality rankings. And when it comes to addressing climate change, 'a worldwide shift to a shorter workweek could cut the CO_2 emitted this century by half', writes Bregman.

How can tourism respond to the growth in migration?

In centuries past, networks of inns and hotels provided beds for pilgrims and refugees fleeing religious persecution across Europe. It is unavoidable that climate breakdown and social fracture will continue to force millions to leave their homes. Acknowledging that our industry networks are by their nature designed to support these people as they seek a better life can reinvigorate the heart of hospitality and should be central to shaping the industry's future.

Thankfully, the earlier mentioned examples of Migrantours and the Magdas Hotel are not the only travel businesses working to help migrants. In 2015, travel agents including the Dutch operator Jonas Madsen granted tourists visiting Greek islands such as Kos and Lesbos an extra 20 kg of free luggage if they used it to take supplies to the refugees arriving there. The Hilton Munich has allocated unused accommodation to welcome refugees, offered them professional training and established a 'Buddy' programme to help them integrate into the city. In 2017, Airbnb launched the Open Homes platform to enable hosts to provide accommodation for refugees, with the price set at zero and Airbnb collecting no fees. TripAdvisor has – along with Google and Microsoft – supported the International Rescue Committee in developing the information portal refugee.info.

In 2016 hotelier Andreas Vasileiou turned over his family-run, seaside hotel on the Greek island of Evia to house refugees and asylum seekers. Responding to a call by the UN Refugee Agency (UNHCR) for Greek hotels to host refugees as part of a programme funded by the European Commission, his hotel now provides a temporary home for up to 88 asylum-seekers from Syria, Iraq, Eritrea and elsewhere. According to the UNHCR:

---

[8] http://www.alastairhumphreys.com/microadventures/ (accessed 31 May 2017).

Fig. 7.1. Syrian refugees cooking in the kitchen at Rovies Hotel. (Courtesy of UNHCR.)

He's created a collective environment where refugees, hotel staff and locals in nearby Rovies village can eat, work and live all together – and learn from each other. At Hotel Rovies, instructors hired through the accommodation programme teach refugees theatre skills and swimming at the beach just outside. Refugee women cook their traditional meals in the bustling collective kitchen, while the reception-area TV blares Arabic channels. Children attend classes in German, English and French, taught by Greek teachers as well as fellow refugees. The community they have built is an example of solidarity in action.

How will global warming change tourism?

The story of this century will be defined by the changing climate and our response to it. What this means is far from clear. We do not know yet what level the temperatures will rise to. We do not know what scale of societal shifts we will make, or be forced to make, in our efforts to meet the challenges. We do not know in full what technological advancements may aid us in this.

It's possible that enough effort will go into reversing our impact on the climate in the years to come to slow down temperature increases considerably and avoid the worst possible outcomes of global warming. It's also possible that more of our efforts will end up being in adaptation towards a more severely climate-altered world. All we know for sure is that the temperatures will continue to rise, and that this is already affecting the liveability of the planet in many ways.

Will ski resorts, already experiencing shortening seasons and impoverished snow conditions, see the lifts continue to run? Will some form of carbon pricing cripple the tourism development of regions reliant on cheap flights? Will the coral reefs that support the livelihoods of millions of people disappear? Will the beaches of the Mediterranean become too hot to sit on? The runways of Dubai too hot to take off from?

How will the tourism industry respond? Will it wait until it is too late? Or will it accelerate its preparations and transform so it might take a leadership role?

Over the last few years, the awkward relationship between tourism, aviation and climate change has made it considerably more challenging trying to develop a coherent, plausible narrative for sustainable tourism. The industry has to do much more than pay lip service to the idea that flying must be significantly reduced, and actively design its future structure to enable it to happen. If it doesn't, the protests of the summer of 2017 will spread, and be joined by divestment campaigns and court cases concerned about the corporate carbon risks contained in their investments.

However, the all-encompassing nature of the issue also presents tourism with an opportunity to rewrite the next chapter in its story as one that gives it a leading role in helping people embrace the changes to come. Hotels are in essence our homes at different scales. All the rooms we might find are there. All the products, the furnishings. The most sustainable of them serve as showcases to their guests as to what is possible. They can also share the knowledge gained as they seek to implement solutions to the various challenges of operating with local citizens, becoming living, immersive incubators and knowledge hubs for sustainable habitation. Difficult to grasp issues such as the circular economy and reversing climate change can be transformed into tangible experiences that people can take pleasure in and experience the benefits of while on holiday.

There are a wealth of ways tourism can reconnect us to the world around us. Some will reinforce the lessons hotels can teach. Some will help interpret our shared pasts. Others can reconnect cultures. And if automation means we have more time at our disposal, but not more money, filling that time in ways that enrich our lives without draining the planet's resources will become essential.

Will we ever reach Shambala?

This book has been an attempt to draw together all the most inspiring, exhilarating initiatives I see around the world to imagine what a positive, transformed future for tourism might look like. Now that it is finished, I'm off to Shambala.

Fig. 7.2. The sun sets over Shambala Festival.

The music at Shambala starts at 3pm on Thursday and carries on until about 4am on Monday morning. Throughout this time there are hundreds of bands, DJs, theatre performances, cabaret acts and more. This annual festival is also a space to explore what our transformed future might look like. This year there was a session on how housing activists took over Barcelona city council (and sought to address overtourism); another on building land-based enterprises and community hubs. There was Wildonomics (10 simple practices to connect humans with nature) and a look at the threat Big Data may have on our privacy. And in case this all sounds rather serious, there's also Drag Queen Bingo and a Run DMC vs Shambala Flashmob.

In 2016 the festival went 100% vegetarian, with the exception of a small experiment in providing insects to eat. All the milk used by the onsite catering is organic. All the tea and coffee is fair trade. All the eggs free range.

Thanks to the meat-free initiative, food waste was reduced by 60 per cent on 2015. In addition, half a tonne of unwanted food was collected from the campers and campervans at the end of the festival, cooked up into meals and redistributed through 180 charitable organisations across Bristol, providing 1055 meals. And because each festivalgoer pays a £2 deposit when they buy their first drink at the bar, last year they saved 1 tonne of plastic waste in four days as a result. All the bars also provide free filtered water, with everyone asked to bring a refillable water bottle.

The festival is 100% powered by renewable energy. A biodiesel shuttlebus connects to the train station and transported 1760 people to the site in 2016. All those who came by car or campervan had to pay a surcharge on their ticket, which was used to fund community solar energy projects in Bristol. Last year £5000 was donated, 'balancing' – to use Shambala's language – 23 tonnes of emissions. Importantly these were balanced in initiatives happening locally and now, rather than planting trees on the other side of the world that would need several years to grow before absorbing carbon. It is, as with Accor, a form of carbon insetting.

I realise that this isn't how everyone wants to pass an August weekend. That doesn't matter. The future in which transformative tourism plays its part will be anything but homogenous. A world of joy, not sacrifice. A few days at Shambala offers an inspiring glimpse into what this life can be.

Further Reading

All the resources I have referenced throughout this book have provided me with valuable insights. However, there is only so much insight that quoting briefly from them in a short book like this can provide. I recommend reading the following in their entirety to anyone interested in developing a transformative tourism industry.

Transforming tourism

- Anna Pollock – *Social Entrepreneurship and Tourism: Setting the Stage* (2016)

Transforming environmentalism

- George Monbiot – *Feral: Rewilding the Land, Sea and Human Life* (2013)
- Paul Hawken – *Drawdown: The Most Comprehensive Plan Ever Proposed to Reverse Global Warming* (2017)

Telling a new story

- Jonah Sachs – *Winning the Story* Wars (2012)
- George Marshall – *Don't Even Think About It: Why our brains are hardwired not to think about climate change* (2014)
- Amithav Ghosh – *The Great Derangement* (2016)

Seeing travel as more than time off work

- Bruce Chatwin – *The Songlines* (1987)
- Jay Griffiths – *Pip Pip: A Sideways Look at Time* (1999); *Wild: An Elemental Journey* (2006)

- Alain De Botton – *The Art of Travel* (2002)
- Tom Hodgkinson – *How to be Idle* (2004); *How to be Free* (2007)
- Rutger Bregman – *Utopia for Realists: And How We Can Get There* (2017)

The problems of mainstream tourism

- Jost Krippendorf – *The Holiday Makers: Understanding the Impact of Leisure and Travel* (1987)
- Leo Hickman – *The Final Call: In Search of the True Cost of Our Holidays* (2007)
- Elisabeth Becker – *Overbooked: The Exploding Business of Travel and Tourism* (2013)

Closing the circle

If you know of arguments, approaches or examples of transformative tourism that would strengthen a second edition of this book, please feed them in. Email me at jeremy@travindy.com or tweet to @jmcsmith to let me know.

Index